*'This is an exceptional book. Newcomers to Gestalt often become somewhat bewildered by its complexity but Bluckert's book provides a straightforward, thought-provoking and practical account of Gestalt, which is comprehensive whilst retaining the subtlety of the approach. It widens the horizons of Gestalt to include teams, organisations and engagement with broader social and political action. It will be required reading on the programmes I deliver. Congratulations. A real achievement'.*

**Dr Geoff Pelham** is a coach, psychotherapist, and educator. He delivers post-graduate coaching programmes and in-house coaching programmes for organisations seeking to develop a coaching style of leadership and management.

*'Gestalt is a powerful and creative approach to human growth and development. In this book Bluckert has brought to life the core principles of Gestalt, their relevance and their impact when coaching individuals and teams. An essential read for any coach or consultant wishing to deepen their practice and understanding of Gestalt'.*

**Gaynor Sharp** is an organisational consultant and executive coach.

*'Psychologically rich, Bluckert's new book is both captivating and highly informative, revealing his in-depth understanding, practice and deep respect for the world of Gestalt. He conveys many of the profound Gestalt principles with clarity and elegance and manages to provide a compelling read whilst also providing a comprehensive overview of this significant field. A must read for coaches and all those in the helping professions, who could not fail to be drawn into the power and excitement of working and, indeed, living this way'.*

**Brigid Garvey** is the co-founder of True North Partnership, a leadership development facilitator, and an executive coach.

# Gestalt Coaching

*Gestalt Coaching: Distinctive Features* makes Gestalt principles, values, and philosophy accessible to coaches of all backgrounds and explains how to apply them in practice.

Peter Bluckert introduces 30 distinctive features of this approach, divided equally between theory and practice. The book provides concise but clear summaries of core concepts such as awareness and contact, the nature and power of unfinished situations, the Field perspective, the phenomenological approach, The Gestalt Cycle of Experience, and the nature of strategic and intimate interactions. Bluckert provides a set of practice guidelines and watch-outs for the Gestalt coach, information on training and development and several case examples to bring the approach to life. *Gestalt Coaching* reveals how this approach can be used in individual development, such as executive coaching, with groups and teams, and in wider social and political contexts.

With a focus on personal growth and development and enhancing co-operation, dialogue, and relationships, this book will be an invaluable tool for coaches of all backgrounds in practice and in training, academics and students of coaching, and anyone interested in learning more about how to apply Gestalt principles in their personal and professional life.

**Peter Bluckert** is founder and chairman of Courage and Spark, a UK-based vertical leadership development consultancy.

# Coaching Distinctive Features
**Series Editor: Windy Dryden**

Leading practitioners and theorists of coaching approaches write simply and briefly on what constitutes the main features of their particular approach. Each book highlights thirty main features, divided between theoretical and practical points. Written in a straightforward and accessible style, they can be understood by both those steeped in the coaching tradition and by those outside that tradition. The series editor is Windy Dryden.

**Titles in the series:**

Cognitive Behavioural Coaching
*Michael Neenan*

Acceptance and Commitment Coaching
*Jon Hill and Joe Oliver*

Psychodynamic Coaching
*Claudia Nagel*

Single-Session Coaching and One-At-A-Time Coaching
*Windy Dryden*

Transactional Analysis Coaching: Distinctive Features
*Karen Pratt*

Gestalt Coaching: Distinctive Features
*Peter Bluckert*

For further information about this series, please visit
www.routledge.com/Coaching-Distinctive-Features/book-series/CDF

# Gestalt Coaching

## Distinctive Features

## Peter Bluckert

LONDON AND NEW YORK

First published 2021
by Routledge
2 Park Square, Milton Park, Abingdon, Oxon OX14 4RN

and by Routledge
52 Vanderbilt Avenue, New York, NY 10017

*Routledge is an imprint of the Taylor & Francis Group, an informa business*

© 2021 Peter Bluckert

The right of Peter Bluckert to be identified as author of this work has been asserted by him in accordance with sections 77 and 78 of the Copyright, Designs and Patents Act 1988.

All rights reserved. No part of this book may be reprinted or reproduced or utilised in any form or by any electronic, mechanical, or other means, now known or hereafter invented, including photocopying and recording, or in any information storage or retrieval system, without permission in writing from the publishers.

*Trademark notice*: Product or corporate names may be trademarks or registered trademarks, and are used only for identification and explanation without intent to infringe.

*British Library Cataloguing-in-Publication Data*
A catalogue record for this book is available from the British Library

*Library of Congress Cataloging-in-Publication Data*
A catalog record has been requested for this book

ISBN: 978-0-367-42981-2 (hbk)
ISBN: 978-0-367-42982-9 (pbk)
ISBN: 978-1-003-00050-1 (ebk)

Typeset in Times New Roman
by Newgen Publishing, UK

# Contents

List of figures and tables ix

Introduction 1

**PART I THEORY: Gestalt principles and key concepts** 5
1. The emergence of a Gestalt coaching approach 7
2. The hallmarks of the Gestalt approach: part 1 11
3. The hallmarks of the Gestalt approach: part 2 17
4. Healthy self-regulation and creative adjustment 21
5. The figure–ground process 25
6. Staying with the 'what is': the phenomenological approach in action 29
7. The Field perspective: the person in context 33
8. Context: balancing the strategic and intimate 37
9. The nature and power of unfinished situations 41
10. Awareness 45
11. Contact, and interruptions to contact 51
12. Ways we interrupt contact, and consequences: part 1 55
13. Ways we interrupt contact, and consequences: part 2 59
14. The Gestalt Cycle as an orienting framework for coaching practice 63

**PART II PRACTICE** 71
15. Creating the conditions for deeper personal development and connection 73
16. The relational stance and dialogic attitude 77
17. Core principles in practice 81

| 18 | Practitioner presence: the intentional use of self | 85 |
| --- | --- | --- |
| 19 | Creative experimentation and improvisation | 91 |
| 20 | Individually focused Gestalt experiments | 97 |
| 21 | Experiments in group and team contexts | 101 |
| 22 | The unit of work as a team learning experiment | 107 |
| 23 | Structured awareness-raising processes in Gestalt coaching | 111 |
| 24 | Support, challenge, and dealing with complexity | 115 |
| 25 | Gestalt-based vertical leadership development programmes | 119 |
| 26 | Resourcing the client: relational know-how for dialogue and effective collaboration | 125 |
| 27 | Practice guidelines for the Gestalt coach: part 1 | 129 |
| 28 | Practice guidelines for the Gestalt coach: part 2 | 133 |
| 29 | Watch-outs for Gestalt coaches | 137 |
| 30 | The training and development of Gestalt coaches | 141 |

| References | 147 |
| --- | --- |
| Index | 150 |

# Figures and Tables

## *Figures*

| | | |
|---|---|---|
| 14.1 | The Cycle of Experience as an orienting framework | 64 |
| 14.2 | The Cycle of Experience as orienting framework (wave representation) | 64 |

## *Tables*

| | | |
|---|---|---|
| 1.1 | The evolution of Gestalt: 1920s to current time | 8 |
| 2.1 | The hallmarks of the Gestalt approach | 12 |
| 8.1 | The elusive balance of strategic and intimate interaction | 38 |
| 9.1 | Examples of psychological tension systems | 42 |

# Introduction

## *Focus of the book*

If you've witnessed the work of a skilled, experienced Gestalt practitioner, you probably noticed a number of things about them. Perhaps you attended a Gestalt therapy or coaching workshop; maybe you were a member of a team working with a facilitator operating from a Gestalt approach; or perhaps you had personal therapy with a Gestalt therapist. You may not be able to put your finger on exactly what struck you, but there was something different about their way of working and being. They seemed to connect with what was happening and had a keen sense of what was needed in the moment. And then, from all the possible interventions available, there was something just right about what they did or said – and the timing of it.

So, if you were able to get inside this Gestalt practitioner's head and witness what they were seeing, what principles were informing their practice, and what theories they were drawing on to make sense of things, what would you learn about the Gestalt approach and method?

This book sets out to provide you with that. The content is presented in two sections – theory and practice – and within that basic structure I address these questions:

## *What would you expect a Gestalt coach to notice and get curious about?*

Examples include: the client's story, content, and context; the 'what is' (current reality) as experienced by the client; their energetic presence; unfinished situations; disowned selves; self-regulation patterns; personal narratives; relational contact patterns/issues; and way of being-in-the-world.

### *What thinking – ideas and concepts – does the Gestalt coach draw on?*

Examples include: the paradoxical theory of change; the Field perspective; systemic thinking; polarities; the Gestalt Cycle of Experience; the meaning of resistance; interruptions to contact; and the strategic/intimate lens.

### *How will the Gestalt approach and methodology reveal itself?*

Examples include: starting from a positive stance and what the person or system is doing well – owning what's well developed before looking for areas of improvement or change; regularly bringing the focus of attention to the here and now; staying close to what's being said, how it's being expressed, how the client is responding and being; sharpening awareness and deepening contact; a process orientation; creative experimentation and improvisation; and the intentional use of self.

### *What will be the qualities of the coaching relationship?*

Examples include: authentic connection; dialogue; conveying openness and transparency; sharing vulnerability and not-knowing; and focusing on contact issues and the dynamic within the coaching relationship.

### *Creating the container: what conditions will the Gestalt coach be seeking to cultivate?*

Examples include: building trust and creating the conditions of sufficient support for deeper personal work; holding the space; and encouraging curiosity and risk-taking.

## *What skills and practices are they likely to be teaching and passing on to clients?*

Examples include the capacity for: self-reflection, deeper self-awareness, dialogue; relational know-how; staying with the process; and expanded perspective-taking.

## *Scope and structure of the book*

The subtitle of this series of short coaching books is 'Distinctive Features', so my task is to provide you with those features of a Gestalt approach to coaching. In keeping with the house-style of this series I will present thirty features in two main sections – Theory and Practice – giving more or less equal weight to each. Some of the chapters are split chapters because the content, even in this abbreviated form, requires more detailed examination than can be realistically handled within a single chapter.

## *Intended readership*

For readers who are unfamiliar with Gestalt, I aim to provide enough detail to give you a real sense and feel for the approach and the mentality. Given the format and style you may want more information, and I will refer you to more detailed Gestalt texts at the end.

The primary focus is on Gestalt coaching with individuals and teams in the organisational context; however, the principles and practices also apply to working in other contexts, such as leadership development programmes, large group interventions, and political and community processes such as citizen's assemblies.

Given the breadth of applications, this book should be relevant to practicing and aspiring coaches, team coaches and facilitators, leadership trainers, internal talent specialists, and learning and development professionals. It should also be of interest to a range of business consultants, and is equally relevant to leaders and managers who want to understand themselves and their colleagues better. Finally, this book should speak to the Gestalt therapist who is transitioning into organisational coaching.

## *What the Gestalt approach can give the coach*

- A body of profound theory and practice that illuminates how the inner journey of personal growth and development happens, and can be assisted
- An approach that helps you to create a more conscious, mindful life for yourself and your clients
- A way of working that includes individual development but is not confined to it. Gestalt practitioners have always been interested in helping individuals heal and self-actualise, but the scope of Gestalt goes beyond this
- The Gestalt approach has much to offer in helping people grow the capacities of co-operation, relationship skill, emotional and ego maturity, and the capacity for dialogue so important in business, politics, and wider life

The emphasis on presence and the intentional use of self invites the coach to fully bring themselves to what they do. From a Gestalt perspective, the coach is the instrument.

# Part I

# THEORY: GESTALT PRINCIPLES AND KEY CONCEPTS

# The emergence of a Gestalt coaching approach

A Gestalt coaching approach finds its theory and practice in four main places: Gestalt psychology; Gestalt therapy where the primary focus has been on individual in-depth work; more recent applications to larger systems such as pairs, couples and families; and organisational consulting where the development of individual leaders, their teams, and the organisation as a whole has been the focus of attention.

Gestalt focuses on people's experience in the present moment (known as phenomenological enquiry), the environmental context or 'field' in which this takes place (the Field perspective), and the creative adjustments individuals and larger systems make to achieve healthy equilibrium and optimal functioning (self-regulation). The Gestalt coach is interested in how their client – be that an individual, group, or team – understands their needs and meets (or fails to meet) them; assists them to better understand their personal process – their habits, behaviours, and relational patterns; and then to choicefully make changes if necessary.

The German word Gestalt, which does not easily translate into English, most nearly approximates to words/terms like 'pattern', 'shape', 'configuration', or 'meaningful organised whole'.

## *Gestalt's main applications*

If you are new to Gestalt your main association may be Gestalt in the clinical context, and until recently this was by far its best-known usage. Gestalt therapy has been practiced since the 1950s, and you

**Table 1.1** The evolution of Gestalt: 1920s to current time

| Gestalt psychology | Gestalt therapy | Gestalt in organisational, family, and community contexts |
| --- | --- | --- |
| Research into perception<br>Figure/Ground process, unfinished situations, self-regulation, creative adjustment, and self-actualisation<br>Field theory | Individual therapy for growth, healing, and wellbeing | Pairs, couples, and family interventions<br>Leadership development, process consulting, vertical development, executive coaching, team coaching, and organisational development (OD)<br>Community development, education, political process, social and ecological change |

can find training institutes and Gestalt therapists all over the world. What's less well known is how Gestalt has been applied in couples and family intervention work, and in non-therapeutic contexts where it has a significant influence on organisation development, leadership development programmes, and coaching. Beyond these contexts, Gestalt has also been applied in political systems, community-building, and social change.

## Gestalt in the organisational context

### Organisational development

It's in the field of organisational development that Gestalt has made some of its most significant contributions, notably through the influence of Kurt Lewin. His vast body of work – which includes field theory, stages of change, group dynamics, action research, sensitivity training, leadership styles, and experiential learning theory – has led many to conclude that Lewin is the seminal figure in the development of OD.

The T-group methodology, which Lewin helped to develop, is an example of the experimental approach in action. The purpose of the workshop experience is to increase awareness of self and others through facilitated group dialogue and feedback. Valuing and appreciating difference is at the heart of the method. Whilst this methodology has grown to be mainstream in management and organisational development, it was a breakthrough in the mid-nineteen-forties when it was founded.

## *Management and leadership development*

Some of the earliest applications of Gestalt within leadership programmes are attributed to Richard Wallen and Edwin Nevis. Beginning in 1959, they used awareness-raising techniques within sensitivity training groups for managers, and this work can be seen as a forerunner of today's workshop-based emotional intelligence and vertical leadership development programmes. Nevis went on to play a leading role in the application of Gestalt principles to organisational consulting, setting up the Organisation Development Centre at the Gestalt Institute of Cleveland in the USA, along with John Carter, Len Hirsch and Carolyn Lukensmeyer, and writing the seminal text on the subject, *Organizational Consulting: A Gestalt Approach* (1987 ). Lukensmeyer went on to bring a Gestalt consulting approach into her governmental work with the US Administration.

## *Process consulting, individual coaching, and team coaching*

Throughout the world, there have been a growing number of Gestalt organisational development practitioners who have taken their own Gestalt styles into process consultancy, team development, mediation, leadership consultation and, more recently, vertical development.

The emergence of a Gestalt coaching approach can be traced to the mid-nineties, though there has never been *one Gestalt OD approach* or *one Gestalt coaching approach*. Rather, a number of templates have emerged depending on the backgrounds of different practitioners. Gestalt therapists moving into the organisational setting have inevitably brought a more in-depth psychological approach to their work, in particular the intrapersonal forces in play. Those coming from organisational development settings have approached the work from different perspectives, paying greater attention to leadership, context, systemic influences, power and hierarchy, relationship, and group dynamics.

## Gestalt in social and political contexts

Since the earliest days of the Gestalt tradition, many of its practitioners have had a strong interest and involvement in social issues, whether they have been practicing as psychotherapists, organisational consultants, coaches, or community activists. Those who have specialised in social and political contexts are often people who care deeply about making a difference at the macro levels of cultural and societal change.

Today, there are numerous Gestalt practitioners, working in diverse continents and countries, and with complex issues such as AIDS reduction, poverty alleviation, political conflict, recovery from trauma, social injustice, and natural disasters. Some of them work through the United Nations or act as advisers to senior government officials, whilst others work through NGOs and more informal networks.

Many have never trained as psychotherapists or Gestalt practitioners. Instead, they have integrated Gestalt principles and methods into their existing professional backgrounds in education, social work, community development, political process, and social activism.

Perhaps this is shaping up to be next-generation Gestalt: the application of a powerful set of principles and an awareness-raising methodology that helps improve relational connection, quality of dialogue, level of co-operation, and more effective collaborative action around critical issues of political and social justice, including the climate and ecological crises. If so, at the broader societal level, it may prove to be Gestalt's most significant and consequential contribution yet – whilst, at the same time, continuing its radical tradition.

# The hallmarks of the Gestalt approach: Part 1

## *The relational stance and the dialogic method*

From a Gestalt perspective, the coaching relationship has certain defining features: inclusion, authenticity, collaborative partnership, strong contact, and dialogue. The Gestalt coach commits to being fully present and offers a quality of relationship grounded in compassion, empathy, and humility. The Gestalt coach works as much from their felt sense – their heart and gut – as from their head.

The capacity to create the conditions for *dialogue* is fundamental to the Gestalt approach. When dialogue is happening, something unpredictable can emerge from those engaged in the interaction. Something previously hidden becomes more visible and better understood that could only have emerged through the sharing of perspectives in a spirit of joint exploration. The outcomes of dialogue can be precious – a deeper sense of connection, new insights, and meaning-making – and are all less likely to be achieved through private reflection because they require engagement and articulation through relationship. Whilst issues remain private and not open to relational dialogue, the prospect of rich, reliable meaning-making can be diminished in both work and wider life contexts.

## *Focusing on 'what is'*

The Gestalt coach pays careful attention to the immediate here-and-now experience and the current reality – the 'what is'. In the coaching

**Table 2.1** The hallmarks of the Gestalt approach

---
The relational stance and dialogic method
Focusing on 'what is'
Awareness
Contact
The Cycle of Experience
Working with emerging process
Practitioner presence and the intentional use of self
Creative experimentation and improvisation
The Field perspective
The paradoxical theory of change
A process orientation
Polarity thinking

---

context, the 'story', content, problems, challenges, and concerns that the client brings are all aspects of the 'what is'. The Gestalt coach is equally interested in *how* the client engages and tells their story, what she's thinking and feeling about the issues being expressed, and what level and variation of energy and connection is present. This includes the level of engagement and contact your client has with you – and you with them. A core Gestalt proposition is that the exploration of here-and-now, direct, felt experience provides constant opportunities for growth and learning.

### *Awareness*

The common ground between most coaching approaches is that awareness-raising is the starting point for growth and change. As people become more aware of their assumptions, belief systems, behaviours, and attitudes they move into a position of choice – to stay with them or to change. The responsibility for this choice lies with them.

Awareness may not automatically lead to change, but it is certainly an essential precursor. People are unlikely to change what they are currently unaware of. However, as their consciousness expands, change becomes possible. This is why all self-development activities and processes are grounded in awareness-raising.

## Contact

From a Gestalt perspective, contact is about being in touch with oneself, others, and the environment in a way which feels strongly connected. Contact does not imply comfortable, affectionate, enjoyable connection, although this is one aspect. Contact can be the delight of hugging your children in a moment of joyful connection; equally, it can be painful and raw when you are grappling with difficult issues. Contact can be fun and playful, and it can be tense and uncomfortable.

To deepen the level of our contact requires that we are more fully present, more awake, and more alive. If you're holding back, going through the motions, or 'managing' the other person, then you're unlikely to be in strong, meaningful contact. Contact is directly related to your level of openness. The challenge to be open requires taking risks, and this can evoke feelings of vulnerability. Neither does reaching out and taking the risk to be vulnerable guarantee the result you're hoping for. The 'other' may not reciprocate, or may not reciprocate how you want them to.

## The Cycle of Experience

Developed by the Gestalt Institute of Cleveland, the Cycle of Experience is an orienting framework for a Gestalt coach. It provides a model for understanding how people satisfy their needs, and achieve resolution and closure (or not) around issues. The Cycle of Experience is represented as an ongoing process, beginning with sensation, and moving through awareness and energy mobilisation to action and contact, followed by resolution, closure, and withdrawal of interest.

Working from a Gestalt approach, much of the early work in a coaching assignment lies at the awareness-raising stage to establish the foundations necessary for developmental work. Learning the art of raising awareness, building trust, and deepening contact are core competencies of the Gestalt coach.

## *Working with emerging process*

Working with emerging process is another hallmark of the Gestalt approach. In this undirected awareness mode, as a coach, you approach your work with as few biases, presumptions, and pre-formed hypotheses as possible. You begin each piece of work from a position of openness to whatever stands out in your client's attention and your own.

This receptive stance allows your interest and curiosity to be captured. It might be as simple as the volume of someone's voice, the strength of their handshake, or the avoidance of eye contact. It might be an engaging vitality, a submissive, apologetic style of relating, or a flatness of energy.

## *Practitioner presence and the intentional use of self*

The intentional use of self is a key notion in Gestalt coaching practice, and it is an advanced level skill. Coaches, as well as their clients, inevitably bring their presence into every context of their lives. The more important question is about how well coaches understand their presence and what it evokes in others (their clients), to what degree their presence is grounded and integrated, and whether they can bring intentionality and variation to it. To do that, you have to know about your presence.

The choices you make as a coach depend on what you believe will be most useful at the time to facilitate goal achievement, growth, and learning. The challenge is to recognise what's needed and seek to provide the presence that will be most appropriate and useful in the moment.

# The hallmarks of the Gestalt approach: Part 2

## *Creative experimentation and improvisation*

In the coaching context, experiments are vehicles to explore the client's experience through active, behavioural, and imaginative expression. They are not a substitute for conversational dialogue, but an extension of it. The aim of an experiment is to expand awareness, understanding, and insight.

Gestalt experiments begin with an idea and then an invitation to *try something*. They are invented through a creative process of dialogue between the coach and the client and with their agreement. The co-creation of the experiment frees up the client to take the initiative whilst also changing the space for the coach to improvise, get creative, and use their imagination and intuition. Whilst they are often enacted within the holding space of an individual coaching session or group-based workshop, they can also be practiced in real-life situations. And, beyond that, one of the goals of Gestalt practitioners is to develop an experimental mindset in themselves and encourage the same in their clients.

## *The Field perspective*

From a Gestalt perspective, we can only ever understand people in their contexts and within their worlds. The way we see and make meaning of our world is something we actively construct. It is unique and personal to each individual, time-relevant, and contextual. It depends on 'figural' conditions such as external pressures and stressors, our needs, our state of well-being, and our interests at any given time. So, whilst we may think of people as relatively unchanging, or even fixed in terms of characteristics, behaviours, and patterns, the Field perspective invites us to consider that our existential states vary and change according to the total situation – or 'life-space', as Lewin called it – which we are currently experiencing and co-creating.

This runs counter to a more individualistic approach where the focus is narrowly on the client alone – their personal challenges, goals, and psychology – and where the bigger 'ecosystem' in which they function can be missed. That ecosystem generates forces that have an enormous effect on who they are in that moment. Change the ecosystem and a different person can begin to emerge.

## *The paradoxical theory of change*

You may have heard a phrase commonly used by experienced practitioners: 'trust the process'. But what does that really mean? To a Gestalt coach it means to trust the paradoxical nature of change: that when people fully embrace their current reality and truth, own and accept it, something alters. This was captured by a participant attending a Gestalt vertical leadership development programme, who said 'I've finally stopped trying to be a person I'm not. Until then, I was always failing'. He was voicing what Beisser (1970) described when people get stuck between who they think they should be and who they think they really are.

From a Gestalt perspective, change can occur by being more of who we are, and when we are fully in contact with 'what is', rather than trying to be different. The Gestalt theory of change, known as the Paradoxical Theory of Change (Beisser, 1970), is based on the assumption that we must first *become our truth* before we can move from it, and the very act of fully exploring and embracing that truth leads to spontaneous self-organisation. A new configuration takes place. As a consequence of this theoretical perspective, the skills and methods used by Gestalt practitioners are intended to create conditions for learning and growth and support people to get in contact, and stay in contact, with 'what is', not what should be.

This deceptively simple proposition is at the core of all Gestalt practice, be that in the coaching, therapy, community-building, or political contexts. It can be a difficult one to take on board for newcomers to the approach, who may believe that something more active is required: a tool, technique, or process. The idea that awareness is ultimately the change agent runs counter to the widely held technical mindset where solutions lie in knowledge, expertise, and making something happen.

## *A process orientation*

Most leaders, managers, coaches, and, for that matter, all of the rest of us live in the world of *task and content* and find it difficult to simultaneously pay attention to *personal, interpersonal, and group process*. Despite often feeling overwhelmed by content, it's the world that professional clients inhabit, and coaches need to both understand and respect that. However, it doesn't have to be the primary focus of the coach. Indeed, this is the place where Gestalt coaches can make their greatest impact: in their capacity to facilitate better process.

## *Polarity thinking*

Polarity theory begins with the proposition that every quality we possess is one end of a continuum, with the opposite quality residing at the other end. We have a capacity to love and hate; offer kindness and be cruel; show warmth yet also freeze someone out; experience happiness and sometimes feel utterly desolate. We may wish to deny the presence of the less virtuous qualities which we see as bad, and we may try to disown them and consign them to what is sometimes described as the Shadow, but they don't magically disappear. On the contrary, under stressful circumstances and when we're exhausted, they often leak out – to our own surprise and disappointment, as well as to others.

We often see only one pole – the opposite pole being invisible to us – and this has consequences for our work as coaches. When one pole is firmly in the light, such as a client who always seems to be cheery and optimistic, we may become blinded to the opposite pole. This may reflect our own preference to show up in the same upbeat way, and could suggest we also have some work to do to own that opposite pole. From a Gestalt perspective, we need to be careful not to reinforce what our clients may already feel about these shadow qualities – that is, that they are entirely negative.

Another important lens on polarity thinking is revealed when we perceive that if A is true, therefore B can't be. This is referred to as *either-or thinking*, and it is commonplace. Expanding our perspective on a whole range of issues typically involves an incorporation of both possibilities – that there can be truth in seemingly opposite or contradictory things. This is referred to as *both-and thinking*.

# Healthy self-regulation and creative adjustment

From a Gestalt perspective, as human beings we have an inherent capacity to stay healthy through effective self-regulation – the natural process of maintaining a balance between gratifying our needs and eliminating tensions. When we meet our needs, and reduce or eliminate tensions, we re-establish a sense of equilibrium; when we don't, there can be a sense of incompleteness and something being unfinished. This can leave us feeling dissatisfied and off balance.

At the physical level this is self-evident. When we feel hungry it becomes an increasingly dominant focus of attention (figure) against the background (ground) of whatever else we are doing at the time. We experience a state of temporary imbalance until that need is met, when it then dissipates with a consequential withdrawal of interest and energy. This process was first described in Goldstein's research (Hall and Lindzey, 1957), where he introduced the concept of self-regulation. According to Goldstein, there is a biological law of balance inherent in human nature, and we are programmed to move towards the best form possible to find that balance. At a later point Goldstein coined the term 'self-actualisation', which he defined as the inherent drive to fulfil one's potential. Maslow, a student of Goldstein, later developed the concept and conducted research into the common characteristics of people he identified as self-actualised.

This perspective takes into account that an individual's equilibrium is in constant flux and can be disturbed by both internal and external phenomena. We exist physically, emotionally, socially, economically, and spiritually in a constant flow between equilibrium and disequilibrium. Changes in our work, family, and social lives, loss of important people, deterioration in health, financial misfortune – these all threaten and disturb our state of being. The nature of how we self-regulate to deal with these challenges is central to Gestalt theory and is one of Gestalt's core organising principles.

Healthy functioning depends on creatively adjusting and adapting to these ever-changing circumstances and presents everyone with the challenge of being aware and attuned to their needs and wants, satisfying them in the most effective ways possible, and learning from experience.

## *Core proposition*

*People are always doing the best they can from how they see, experience and make sense of the world, and taking into consideration their personal histories.*

This proposition arises out of the concept of creative adjustment: that people make the best decisions and alter their behaviour towards the best outcomes available within the external constraints acting on them, and their own internal perceptions of what is possible at any given time. This doesn't mean that those decisions and actions will always be helpful or impact positively on others. They are simply the best people can do, with their current level of awareness, within their circumstances and the broader context of their life.

## *More complex needs*

Clearly, when it comes to more complex psychological and emotional needs – and the decisions that can emerge from these – our capacity to self-regulate is more challenged. For some people, knowing what they want and need, can be elusive. And when we factor in the complexities of our personal histories in relation to meeting some of our most important needs, we begin to really appreciate what's meant by this proposition.

## *Self-regulation patterns*

From our earliest years, and as we grow, we learn to find solutions to the problems in front of us. How we do that, and how healthy our creative adaptations are, will be influenced by our environments. As youngsters, were we encouraged to try things out, take risks, make mistakes, and learn? Were we left to our own devices too much, or were we overly-protected? Did we grow up in family environments where feelings were expressed or repressed? Were we comforted and held, or did we have to find our own ways of self-soothing? Did we experience affection and grow up believing we are lovable and deserving of love? Was there sufficient support for our emerging identity, our difference and personhood?

We self-regulate in the context of our environment and the level of support we expect to find there. This sets the scene for the self-regulating patterns we develop over our lives. Some of these continue to serve us well; others less so. They made sense at the time but are now outdated and restrictive.

Personal growth agendas often lie in this space: identifying these unhelpful patterns, re-evaluating them, and learning to deconstruct those that have become fixed Gestalts – that is, overly rigid ways of responding to the world.

Such patterns often manifest in our bodies, our ways of looking after ourselves (or lack of self-care), and the intimacy of our relationships. The individual who never really knew love and affection as a child may have built a protective armour around themselves and find it very difficult in the present time to allow love in, despite being in a committed relationship.

## *The issue of support*

It's not really possible to appreciate people's existential states and self-regulation patterns, healthy or otherwise, without understanding how much or how little environmental support has been available to them in their lives. And whether they have felt able to draw on that support or, instead, developed a pattern of over-reliance on self-support.

These questions and issues will manifest in the coaching relationship and the nature of the contact between yourself as coach and your client. From a Gestalt perspective, the same questions and issues are just as relevant to you as coach, and will also show up in your contact style.

## *Triumphs*

When I hear the stories of people's lives, and what they have had to confront at various stages of their life experience, what stands out is the extraordinary courage and creativity they've employed to get themselves through. Listening to them, one can only conclude that these are stories of triumph. Rarely, however, do they see it this way – or at least not until their awareness is heightened around what they have had to deal with, how well they've responded, and what they have achieved.

# The figure–ground process

## *Needs organise our field of perception*

Gestalt takes a needs-based approach to understanding human functioning and behaviour. Kurt Lewin's (1952) research demonstrated that our needs, and the tensions that arise out of them, influence both what we perceive and what we act on. Our perceptual process is not random; it is structured and contains meaning. Certain things stand out at any given time for a reason. For example, if you have a young family you start to notice the routes and public facilities that are most child-friendly and those which are difficult to negotiate. Beforehand you probably didn't notice any of this. If you fracture a leg and need to use crutches you will quickly become aware of which buildings have easy access and which don't. If you're planning to buy an electric car, you start to notice them on the roads and where the charging points are.

Lewin captured the essence of this in the following way: emerging needs (*figures*, in Gestalt language) organise our perception of the field and our engagement within it. We see what we need to see and what is both important and relevant to us at the time – and this is one of Gestalt's core organising principles.

A *figure* is whatever occupies the foreground of your interest right now. It might be a sensation, a thought, or a feeling. It might be a challenge to overcome, or an issue that you're worried about. A *figure* can be what you are looking at, listening to, or playing with. It's whatever is occupying your attention right now.

What's figural to you can be exciting or pleasing or, equally, it may cause you irritation or anxiety. If you've ever been a participant in a Gestalt workshop you may have been asked by the facilitator 'So, what's figural for you right now?' They were inviting you to describe what was *on top* for you at that time. The well-used group-work exercise known as the *check-in* has a similar purpose – to surface what's important in the moment and begin to make connection. Similarly, many professionals in the fields of psychotherapy, counselling, and social work are taught early in their training to *start where the client is* – essentially with what's figural.

In a literal sense, *ground* is everything else: the internal and external world that for the moment is not in the foreground of your attention. Ground is the context from which figures emerge. In a deeper sense your *ground* includes your worldview, your ways of seeing and acting in the world, your habitual patterns, your beliefs, values, and assumptions, your mental frameworks, all of which shape the way you construct your reality. Some of this is visible and available to you (conscious) and some of it isn't. This bedrock, your experiential ground, is the lens that filters what you see and don't see, and how you make sense of new events or *figures*.

If, for example, your *ground* includes a belief that you can never understand complex theories, then you might quickly give up on learning new concepts. Similarly, if you have always believed that you cannot do sport then you might subsequently avoid opportunities to try out new physical activities. And if you received regular criticism when you were young, as an adult you may now struggle to hear feedback because you interpret anything negative as criticism or attack. In other words, our *ground* has a major bearing on how we relate to current *figures* and can be the source of much confusion, misinterpretation, and misunderstanding. In simple terms, it's what causes our buttons to be pressed.

### *Examples of common figures brought to coaching conversations*

- Current challenges, problems and issues
- Unmet needs

- Dilemmas with no right answer or solution
- Relationship issues
- Existential challenges, such as loneliness, unhappiness, fear, uncertainty, loss of confidence, identity, or purpose
- Unresolved historic issues and unfinished business
- Feeling overwhelmed and stressed by a level of complexity beyond one's existing capacities
- Insufficient support of the kind needed

## *Resolving today's issues versus transformational change*

Dealing with today's issues and problems is important in providing help with challenges, decisions, and actions. This is the problem-solving dimension to coaching. In the bigger picture, however, transformational learning and development requires a change in *ground*, the substance of who we are, not simply the resolution of today's current issues (*figures*). Otherwise, people may be consigned to the very same figures returning over and over again, and acting out self-defeating patterns of behaviours. This explains why transformational development requires working at greater depth and over a longer period.

# Staying with the 'what is': The phenomenological approach in action

## The phenomenological approach

Working phenomenologically requires that you stay as faithful as possible to the obvious, such as the actual words used, energetic presence, mood, body language, and feeling states. You're tuning in, as far as possible, to what your client is getting in touch with, and this is founded on the belief that there is inherent wisdom in direct, felt experience. You're also interested in how your client self-organises and manages himself and his life – how he scares and settles himself, takes on challenges or avoids them, feels compelled to stay strong or allows his vulnerability. You're curious about how he really feels about himself, deep down, and how he looks after himself (or not).

Working from this standpoint requires a stronger focus on description than interpretation and analysis. It also requires well-honed observational skills that enable you to notice what is right there in front of you. This, in short, is the phenomenological approach in action.

## Stay with 'what is'

The starting point for Gestalt inquiry is always to thoroughly explore the *what is* – that is, the current reality. Whether you're looking at yourself, or reality as experienced by the 'other' ('other' can mean an individual, a group or team, a couple, a family, etc.), begin with what exists, what is real, rather than with some arbitrary notions of what *should be*. Help people to discover and speak the truth of their experience.

Support both polarities and don't favour positive states and emotions over those that don't feel so good or that seem difficult. If you overly support the positive polarity, you inadvertently make it more likely that the person will repress the other. Try to suspend judgement and let the story emerge. Don't rush to premature interpretations, problem-solving, or action plans. Resist the urge to *move on*, a behavioural pattern so prevalent in corporate life, and replace it with *let's stay where we are and deepen things* until the issues are clearer and can be properly understood and dealt with. Then let's move on.

### *Stay with the here and now*

Awareness is always present time. You can anticipate and worry about the future, you can reminisce about the past, but you are always doing these things in the present moment. The here and now is where life occurs, and learning to live mindfully in the present moment is a cornerstone of the Gestalt approach. Describing and sharing the 'what is', becoming more aware and in contact, engaging in dialogue – all of these can only occur in the 'now'. When we share our hopes, plan ahead, feel regrets about the past, we do all of these things in the present moment. Staying *here and now*, focused and striving to explore and deepen contact in the experiential moment rather than analyse, conceptualise, and rationalise, are key features of the Gestalt approach. Translated into the Gestalt method, this means looking for every opportunity to move the conversation from *talking about* current reality to more fully *experiencing it* in the present moment. This in turn ensures that the coaching conversation is addressing the real and actual concerns and priorities of the client, rather than what they think they should be thinking and talking about, as defined by others.

This stance doesn't ignore the importance of past events. Indeed, one of Gestalt's most important contributions is the understanding of unfinished business, its impact, and how we can work with it. From a Gestalt perspective, however, what is important is not the past event per se; rather, it is the effect it's having in the present situation. If, for example, I had a negative experience with a previous boss which I was unable to gain closure around, then I may treat my current boss with distrust and keep my distance. By increasing my awareness in the present moment, I may discover and learn more about how my current behaviour has echoes of my past. My behaviour becomes more meaningful to me and I recognise that actually my current boss is quite a different individual, the circumstances are significantly different, and I don't need to replay an old pattern.

## *Helping individuals and groups become here-and-now focused*

So, how can we help individuals and groups become here-and-now focused? This is most obviously achieved by asking questions which raise awareness. Examples would be: 'What are you aware of right now?'; 'What do you notice in yourself and others?'; 'What do you want to know or ask, here and now?'; 'What do you want?'; 'How will you go about getting what you want?'; 'What is happening for you right now as you speak about this?'

All of these questions share some common factors. The first is that they are 'how' and 'what' questions. 'Why' questions tend to take people into explaining and justifying themselves, which may not lead to heightened awareness and contact. The second is that they are present tense. They are located in the 'now' and are likely to produce more direct contact with immediate thoughts, feelings, and needs.

In addition to asking questions, it is helpful to prefix statements with the pronouns 'I' and 'you', rather than 'it', 'her' or 'him'. In groups and teams, it is common for group members to refer to someone else in the room as 'he', 'she', 'him' or 'her', rather than speaking directly to the person and using the pronoun 'you'. This communication style can leave the person feeling as if they don't exist. Another outcome of the third-person relating pattern is that it keeps things more psychologically distant. The other person is at arm's length – beyond the range at which meaningful contact can happen.

Groups and individuals who are rarely asked the sorts of questions listed above (such as 'What are you aware of now?') will sometimes experience some initial confusion. They feel that they have been put on the spot – asked for an answer that they don't seem to have. Part of the reason for this is that they go looking for a deep and meaningful motivation behind the question. They over-complicate it. Instead of noticing the obvious, what is right there in front of them, they dismiss that as not sufficiently important. Instead, they embark on a futile mission of trying to discover what lies under the stone rather than what is sitting on the stone. Awareness training then becomes part of the process, helping people see what's on the stone and to use their full range of senses.

# The Field perspective: The person in context

Our contexts make a world of difference to our sense of who we are, our well-being, optimism, and self-efficacy. In the organisational context, for example, this is the rationale for seeking to create developmental organisations. The extent to which team and organisational cultures are enabling or disabling, supportive or undermining, plays a huge part in people's levels of engagement and personal motivation, and whether they fulfil their potential – irrespective of personal characteristics such as desire, drive, and ambition.

The Field, or context, shapes and creates us, just as, conversely, we shape and co-create it.

## *The Field perspective*

*'Human beings never exist as psychological entities in isolation – they come entwined with their systems, beliefs, traditions, and cultures... we need to think like social ecologists and look at people in their contexts. If people are to change, then so also must the conditions and contexts of their lives. We are not only in contexts, we are part of them. Moreover, we act as contexts for others – we help make up their worlds'*

*– Parlett (2015).*

Field theory is based on the proposition that everything is related, is in constant change and flux, and has an impact on everything else – whether we can see it in the moment or not. Sometimes, we can see it: for example, behaviour and social interaction. On other occasions, it may be less clear, such as mood, subtle changes in body language or quality of engagement. And then there are the times when we just sense something and don't quite know what it is.

Inspired by the work of Kurt Lewin, one of the founders of Organisation Development (OD), the Field perspective can be described as an *outlook* and *a way of thinking* about the interconnectedness between events and the settings or situations in which they take place. It invites you to look at the *total situation* and take a holistic perspective on the wider influences at play in all human interactions. This stands in contrast to the more individualistic perspective of viewing problems, issues, and symptoms as if they exist in isolation – simply as part of a person's character and personality.

It was Lewin's contention that behaviour is a function of the person and the environment together – one constellation of independent factors which he called the 'lifespace' of the individual.

The Gestalt coach therefore seeks to understand their client's experience in relation to the complexities of their whole situation, which in turn requires the coach to appreciate issues arising out of levels of systems beyond the individual level. For example, in the organisational coaching context, adopting a Field perspective means that you will be interested in external challenges and changes, political considerations, leadership, hierarchy, power, status, and inclusion/exclusion.

### *Felt sense as the royal road*

Looking inwards and learning to access your 'felt sense' – a body sensation that is meaningful – as Gendlin (1978) called it, also provides you with access to the Field.

Working with felt sense invites you to notice your emotional state and mood, energy and excitement, reluctance and resistance, flow and stuckness, and the subtle shifts that are always happening. It is an invitation to pay attention to the full range of your senses, which helps you become more receptive to the wisdom of your body.

When you focus on your felt sense you might become more aware of stomach flutters or a dryness in the throat as you start to speak, or a heaviness in your heart as you think of a loved one who is troubled or struggling. Gendlin suggested that a felt sense is often experienced in the middle of the body – the abdomen, stomach, chest, and throat in particular – although a felt sense can also occur in other parts of the body. Felt senses are different from emotions, although they are likely to contain emotions. If emotions are like primary colours, felt senses are like subtle blends of colours. The emotion might be 'fear', but the felt sense of that fear would be jumpiness or feeling slightly sick. Felt sense is your guide to your readiness to engage and your emotional tone at any particular time. It's your body's 'truth'.

# Context: Balancing the strategic and intimate

## *Appreciation of organisational context*

Irrespective of whether you are coaching in business, non-commercial, political, or community contexts, it's essential to have a strong appreciation of both strategic and intimate forms of relationship. Nevis, Backman, and Nevis [2003] defined strategic interactions as 'the ways in which individuals exchange influence when the goal is to accomplish a specific task. Achieving the goal is of primary importance and, though connectedness is still desired, mutuality gives way to getting something done.' Intimate interactions, on the other hand, are defined as 'those which bring us closer to each other through caring about what each person is thinking and feeling. The intent is to enhance connectedness as a desirable goal in its own right.'

Strategic interactions are typically the prime focus and the most valued in the corporate world. However, it's clear that there will always need to be a balance of some kind, and many corporate leaders and leadership teams recognise the need to pay attention to both strategic and intimate interactions. Over time, the balance will shift according to circumstances, but when it's at its optimum it can lead to higher levels of commitment and performance, as well as improved personal well-being and satisfaction.

I have presented Table 8.1 to many senior leaders and their teams, and they often say 'despite knowing better, we focus far more on the left side (of the two columns), and we need to be more on the right. We haven't got the correct balance'. With good intentions,

**Table 8.1** The elusive balance of strategic and intimate interaction

| Strategic | Intimate |
| --- | --- |
| Focus on getting things done (task accomplishment) | Focus on how people are |
| Business results and success is what matters | Well-being of individuals and team is what matters |
| Performance focus | People and relationship focus |
| Caring about outcomes | Caring about people |
| Cognitive intelligence (IQ) and analytical, rational thinking | Emotional intelligence (EQ) and expression of feelings |
| Action plans and to-do lists | Expanding awareness and promoting insight |
| The intentional use of hierarchy, power, and authority – sizing up | Deliberately reducing role power, hierarchy, and authority – sizing down |
| Formality | Informality |
| Being considered, careful, measured, and calculated (political) | Being more open, sharing feelings and exposing vulnerability (non-political) |
| Staying protected, keeping a distance, and keeping people out | Letting your guard down and letting people in |

they commit to re-balancing, but what's intriguing is that it so often proves difficult to translate the insight into sustained change. In most business-as-usual situations, the right-hand side disappears from view and becomes background.

Clearly, some of the explanation for this lies in the cultural norms and expectations of the organisation. The hectic pace and considerable pressures of executive environments also partly explain it. And how realistic is it to ask organisational leaders to be more real and authentic when at the same time they're expected to hold secrets, manage boundaries, and terminate people's jobs? For many senior managers, this prompts the question 'how close do I really want to get to my people?'

In turn, the team members directly reporting to that senior leader will be aware that a certain level of compliance and loyalty is expected of them. So, it's only savvy to 'play the game' and learn to read the organisational politics.

It's important that the coach brings the ability to work with the organisational context, and the needs of the client, rather from their own preferences. A Gestalt approach might appear synonymous with the more contactful intimacy agenda. However, experienced coaches working at the senior leadership level come to recognise the importance of balancing the strategic with the intimate in line with the 'what is'. There will be times when their individual coaching clients need to creatively adapt to the strategic agenda to protect themselves. This can take various forms, such as compromising; holding one's thoughts and feelings to oneself; carefully choosing one's moment to say things; turning away from some conflicts; and, on occasions, backing down and waiting for a better time. It can also mean hunkering down to buy time to manage one's exit and find another career opportunity elsewhere.

HR directors and talent directors have become ever-more sophisticated and discerning in their choice of external coaches and appreciate the added value of a coach who brings both lenses and skill-sets: the strategic and the intimate. They know that their internal client, for example the CEO, may wish to talk to their coach about the implications of a new merger and share their strategic thinking about the opportunities and threats inherent in the situation. Within the same conversation they may also reflect on personal anxieties or issues they have with their chairman.

### *Where the balance is in favour of the intimate*

Though it may seem unlikely that a company culture would consistently pay greater attention to the intimacy agenda, they do exist. As a coach, you may have experienced this yourself if you have been part of a consultancy firm which has prized its level of relational connection, team ethos, and informal, non-hierarchical culture. When the possibility of a community of practice with like-minded colleagues exists, it can be a very attractive proposition. And when that support is generously given by colleagues, the business agenda can suddenly become less interesting.

If this kind of group were to look at the two-column chart shown in Table 8.1 they might have quite the opposite reaction to the one described when most corporate leadership groups see it. They may come to the conclusion that they have become so focused on the right-hand side, the intimacy agenda, that they've lost sight of the left-hand side, the strategic. And if they are in business together, as opposed to being a peer support group, then there may be serious consequences for the business.

# The nature and power of unfinished situations

Our lives are laden with unfinished situations; it's simply part of life that new tasks and challenges arise and, as quickly as we complete them, others naturally follow in their wake. We perpetually live with uncompleted jobs and projects, many of them relatively trivial. At the same time, we also carry more significant unfinished material around major life events and situations. In this chapter I explore the nature of unfinished situations and how the enduring power of unfinished business from the recent and distant past can result in illness, drain energy, interrupt focus, affect motivation, and reduce contact. I also make the connection with how it can hold us back from seeking out new possibilities, fulfilling our potential, and attending fully to the business of living.

## *Unfinished situations as sources of tension*

Gestalt psychologists were interested in the whole aspect of unfinished business as a source of tension in the self-regulation process. Bluma Zeigarnick's (1927) research showed that unfinished actions and situations were better remembered than finished ones and produce what came to be known as 'tension systems'. When people are unable to effectively regulate their tension system and achieve resolution, there can be negative consequences for their health, well-being, and vitality. Table 9.1 presents just a few examples of psychological tension systems. You'll notice that whilst

**Table 9.1** Examples of psychological tension systems

---

Powerful feelings arising from historic unfinished situations

Recurring memories of traumatic situations

Loss and imminent loss

A broken heart

Difficult questions that don't go away

A feeling of going around in circles

A dilemma or difficult decision yet to be resolved

An anxiety-provoking conversation yet to happen

Feeling unable to act because the timing is wrong, the situation is complex, and we don't want to make a mistake

Having to wait on a decision or event elsewhere that impacts our life in a significant way

---

some emanate from the past, most of these unfinished situations are present-time issues.

## Tension as a source of energy and motivation

Any and all of these have the potential to immobilise people and produce a sense of stuckness. When they are present, and especially when they carry a strong emotional charge, it produces discomfort, and the natural reaction is to want them to go away. People sometimes refer to putting their unresolved issues into boxes and hiding them away. It's an example of creative adjustment – the best they can do at the time.

To compound things further, there will always be new needs competing for attention, some of which may be too complex and emotionally loaded for people to reach closure sequentially or speedily. They may contain high levels of significance, such as when we feel let down by a colleague or we fail to land a job that we believed was ours by right.

## Coaching conversations often reveal unfinished business

In the work context, unfinished business is a critical factor in both individual and team performance, yet because there is rarely enough support to face into it, a belief can take root that it's not even possible or worth trying. People come to the conclusion that they just have to learn to live with it or leave. Every day, competent, high-achieving people leave their jobs due to unresolved issues with their organisations, typically around their relationship with their boss. Some teams are sinking under the weight of historic unfinished business.

Understandably, the prospect of addressing unfinished business is daunting to many people. They fear that if they lift the lid, the floodgates will open. On the other hand, just as crises can provide the opportunity for change, unfinished situations and the tensions arising from them can provide a source of energy and fuel for change when people feel able to face them.

A very common emotional 'figure' in the workplace is the issue of inclusion, yet many people go through prolonged periods of feeling devalued, ignored, or side-lined by their boss or the organisation. When this happens, their energy can be stuck on a negative focus. This is an example of an unfinished situation or 'unfinished business'. Although people can tolerate the existence of a number of unclosed experiences, if and when they become compelling enough, they can generate self-defeating activity and demand closure.

## The coach's unfinished business

One of the reasons that deeper personal development work is such a demanding and challenging space for the coach is that there is often two levels of unfinished business operating in the room at the same time. The first is the material that's surfacing in the client; the second is the coach's unfinished business being evoked and restimulated by bearing witness.

Melnick and Nevis (2018) listed the following as some of the most common responses from their students on Gestalt programmes when asked to notice signs of their own unfinished business when working with others:

- Feeling overly responsible for their clients
- Experiencing exhaustion
- Experiencing unusually strong physical reactions
- Only seeing one client and not the system
- Giving unsolicited advice or going into 'download mode' with theoretical explanation
- Reacting too quickly or over-reacting

Experienced coaches working with individuals and teams are likely to recognise some of these signs and know that they are telling us something about ourselves. They are classic coaching supervision issues and valuable to our growth and learning.

## *Some things just don't stay quiet forever ...*

*'All experience hangs around until a person is finished with it'. Polster and Polster (1973).*

A coaching client expressed it this way:

*'I hit a point where I needed to get on, once and for all and sort myself out – address the stuff that has served me well in some aspects – getting on professionally – but has also been disastrous personally. To be the person I want to be, I have to address these past things.'*

## Awareness

Awareness is our route into understanding ourselves, others, and the relationships between us. It's the foundation of emotional intelligence, our capacity to self-manage and self-regulate. This means that the coach needs to appreciate the primary place of awareness-raising in the coaching process and how to facilitate it.

A core Gestalt proposition is that heightened awareness is the key to learning, growth, and development. Growth and development occur when people expand what they can see, have choice about, and can act on. This empowering proposition is at the core of all personal development approaches and, from a Gestalt perspective, starts with sharpening awareness.

This emphasis on awareness as the change agent means that the Gestalt coach needs to learn to be an *awareness-raising partner*. What clients go on to do (or not do), the decisions they make, and the actions they take are the business of the client, not the coach. As such, the role of coach as expert, problem-solver, and fixer is not compatible with the Gestalt approach.

The concept of awareness needs to be differentiated from insight, which is usually understood as temporary 'aha!' experiences where new thinking and mental connections take place. Awareness, on the other hand, is an ongoing process, available at all times, and derives from our whole range of body sensations and mental and emotional experiences. More specifically, this includes what we see, hear, smell, and touch in addition to our thoughts and feelings. It also includes our capacity to be aware of our awareness.

The often-used Gestalt question 'What are you aware of now, as you tell me this?' is intended to bring the person into the here-and-now and move the conversation from the story-telling level to what the individual is in touch with, their sensations, feelings, and new insights. Newcomers to the Gestalt approach often mistake the intention and think that this question is really asking 'What are you feeling right now?' Not necessarily so. There are obviously times when the question refers to the emotional experience of the client; however, this generic awareness question is purposefully undirected. In other words, it enables the client to answer it any way they want. They may recall some memories, tell you what they're thinking about right now, or possibly share a felt sense of being aware of physical tension. The invitation to share across the full range rather than being guided towards feelings in particular can be a relief to some people – especially those who struggle to describe what they feel.

## *Self-awareness*

I invite you to first consider your awareness at the physical/bodily level. Ask yourself 'What am I aware of in my body right now?' Do you notice any physical sensations, such as hunger, an itch, an ache, or a low level of tiredness or discomfort? When you are excited or anxious, what are you aware of in your body: a knot in your stomach, dryness of mouth? Notice your breathing and whether it's shallow or deep.

Now consider what you see around you in the room in which you are reading this book. Or, if you are sitting outside, take in the environment around you. What stands out for you? Don't analyse it, just notice it. Similarly, what can you hear – a clock ticking, someone hoovering in the next room, the hum of the computer? Again, if you're outside notice the sounds of the birds, the traffic passing by, a dog barking. Take in the aromas in your environment. We don't often take the time to notice all of this. Now, take another moment and take stock of your thoughts. What are your thoughts right now? Are you thinking 'This is quite interesting', or perhaps 'Where's all this leading?', or 'Yes, but all this is obvious'. Notice your thinking for a while. When you're ready, look into yourself and discover what you are feeling right now. Are you happy, content, enjoying the moment? Are you bored, frustrated, disappointed?

These are just starters for what you can be aware of. When you are in the normal run of things, take a moment to observe your inner dialogue, the voice inside you which is planning, making lists, dreaming, fantasising, worrying, or trying to remember something.

Notice your 'negative' feelings, such as anger, fear, shame, jealousy, and loneliness, and also your 'positive' ones, such as love, affection, warmth, and compassion. Ask yourself whether you attach the labels 'positive' and 'negative' to them and whether this is helpful.

## *Social awareness*

Most of what I've covered up to this point lies within the realm of internal awareness. Now, let's take a look at what we can become aware of at the interpersonal and social levels. We spend much of our time with other people in one–one, small-group, and larger group situations. How much do we notice of what's going on around us and between us? Here is a top-level view of what we can be aware of in our social interactions.

Firstly, we can become more attuned to communication. Take the example of a workplace meeting: how much engagement, energy, and interest appear to be in the room? What are people doing? Are they looking at each other, listening, or playing with a laptop, off in another world? Who talks, and who doesn't? Who has impact, and who hasn't? Is the atmosphere dull and lethargic, or fun and energised? What are people's communication styles and patterns? One person may talk forever, averaging three or four minutes each time they speak. Another may pipe up with a quirky, short remark every now and then. Do some people deflect, switch off, get irritated? Does anyone try to facilitate a better process? Is 'difference' acknowledged or denied? Is conflict encouraged or suppressed? How does leadership operate? What is the level of emotional intelligence being displayed in the room? How are different people 'playing' the power dynamics?

And, of course, this is just the tip of the iceberg in terms of what we can be aware of in our social interactions. But if we want another direct route into relational awareness, all we need to do is to stop and think about times when we've experienced a lack of awareness on the part of someone in our lives. How did you feel when someone you care about failed to see when you really needed something from them, or saw it and ignored your needs? How do you feel when you listen to someone talking at length about themselves but not reciprocating and asking how you are?

### *The coach's self-awareness*

The coach's self-awareness is a critical factor in working competently in the Gestalt approach. This means:

- Noticing the extent to which you're fully present
- Being aware of how available you are for connection
- Noticing whether you are reaching out, and allowing your client to reach in to you
- Standing back from your own experiences and reflecting on your moods, behaviours, and your current level of optimism or pessimism
- Noticing when you're triggered by your own material and restimulated, and how you may be acting this out in unhelpful ways
- Suspending judgement about another person's reality as they see it and experience it

Recognise your familiar patterns around such themes as self-doubt, submission or aggression, the need to be liked or to be at the centre of things, to bask in your knowledge of latest theories, or name-drop to feel important. Equally important if you're coaching executives, what are your characteristic reactions to power, status, and hierarchy?

## *Does this all suggest we need to constantly live at a heightened level of awareness?*

Whilst from a Gestalt perspective awareness is central to healthy functioning, good connection with others, and personal growth, we don't need to be in a heightened state of awareness all of the time to self-regulate effectively. On the contrary: much of our time is spent without much awareness of what's going on internally, in other people around us or in the wider environment. Our survival mechanisms and our everyday behaviours happen in a habitual way, requiring only a minimal level of awareness. We sometimes refer to this state as being on automatic pilot. If it were to be measured on a gauge, it may fluctuate between 2 and 5 on a scale of 1–10 for much of the time, and that's just about enough for many of our routine activities. The problem is that the dial can get stuck at this level and we find that we are living our lives at a relatively low level of personal and social awareness.

Where this really matters is when we consider the issue of personal growth and development, because awareness is essential to living mindfully and with choice and responsibility. As Melnick and Nevis (2018, p. 78) put it, 'Becoming aware is an awakening; an awakening that is often energising'. It often arrives with a new sense of possibilities. This explains the euphoric feeling some people get when experiencing a breakthrough coaching session, or in a personal growth workshop, when their awareness level significantly changes upward to 8 or 9: they feel as if a light has been switched on, they can see more, and they feel more alive.

# Contact, and interruptions to contact

Engagement, connection, knowing what you're in touch with, and letting things in are what defines contact; enhanced contact is a primary goal of Gestalt coaching. Contact can be understood in terms of a person's connection to themselves, others, and their environment. The extent to which individuals are genuinely present and engaged reflects their levels of contact. When a person goes deeper into themselves, connects strongly with others, or more vividly experiences the world right in front of them, they experience a different quality of contact. When that happens they often want to spend more of their life in that space. It's as if there's been an awakening, an opening up, and they want to hold onto it. They have rediscovered their spark. It follows, therefore, that an important aspect of their personal development journey will be to discover ways to stay awake, open, alive, in contact. It may also involve learning how they interrupt contact with themselves, with others, and with the world around them.

We have a multitude of ways we do this; these can include denial, desensitising, deflecting, projecting onto others, staying over-busy, numbing-out, and more. Consciously, and unconsciously, we know how to shut down, and sometimes we need to do that. The problem arises when this becomes habitual and we can't find our way back to more fluid, in-the-moment responses which more accurately match the situation.

## *What we can be in contact with*

Contact is seen as a relational process referring to our contact with ourselves, our contact with the environment and our contact with other people. Notice that in all three spaces the important common words are 'contact with …'.

So, what can we be in contact with? The three most obvious answers to this question are: we can be in contact with ourselves; we can be in contact with the environment, the world around us; and we can be in relational contact with others.

If we take the meaning of contact as *knowing what we are in touch with at any given moment* it should make it simple, obvious, for us to know a great deal about the nature of our contact with ourself, our connection with the world right in front of us, and with the people in our lives. Yet, very often it isn't. It's not at all unusual for people to struggle with knowing what they're sensing, thinking, and feeling. We can walk through the most beautiful scenery on a fine day and hardly notice it. We can be with our closest loved ones and yet be barely connected. So, what's happening here? Are we elsewhere, with our busy minds? Is our internal dialogue preoccupying us to the extent that we're hardly listening; instead, are we making lists, worrying over recent things we said or did? How much of the time are we really present, open, receptive, and noticing what's around us?

Relationally, there's another important element. Relational contact is not simply dependent on whether you are open and prepared to be impacted by the other; it's also about the extent to which you are reaching out to others, going towards the world, and taking the psychological and emotional risks of being in contact.

## *Contact–withdrawal patterns*

We all have our unique contact–withdrawal patterns. Some people thrive on all-out, full-on, contactful, relational living. They search it out and it's the lifeblood of their experience. Others need regular periods of withdrawal before being ready to re-engage. Withdrawal doesn't necessarily suggest withdrawal from all contact; it might be that a person feels the need to withdraw from intense relational contact to deepen their contact with themselves through reflection, meditation, or connection to nature, music, or the arts.

It can be helpful to become more attuned to your own contact/withdrawal rhythms and patterns and become aware of the contact styles of significant others in your life. Equally, notice your own familiar ways of interrupting contact both with yourself and with others. Have you developed the habit of making a quick, smart comment or joke which can act as a deflection from the seriousness of a situation? This may be useful at times to alter the mood in the room, but done too often can leave other people feeling irritated or frustrated.

## *Interruptions to contact*

From a Gestalt perspective, interruptions to contact can be seen as an expression of 'creative adjustment' – habits and patterns of people doing the best they could to initially solve a problem or adapt as best they could to their world. Starting from here, the Gestalt practitioner adopts a respectful, non-judgemental stance in their work not simply as a better tactical decision or because it raises less resistance, but also as a philosophical position. To work from a Gestalt approach is to take a more optimistic view, emphasising what the individual (or system) is doing well. People do not interrupt contact without a reason. Interruptions will be meaningful within the context of either the present or the individual's life history, or a mixture of both. If I have had painful experiences in the past when I have spoken out against power figures, I may have learnt to creatively adjust by keeping my thoughts and feelings to myself (retroflecting). If I am now working in a management culture that does not support the expression of difference, I may replay my pattern of retroflecting and keep my head beneath the parapet for fear of looking bad or being ridiculed or bullied.

The trouble with interruptions to contact is that, for the most part, they are unconscious, outside of our awareness, and may relate far more to the past than the present. They have become habitual patterns and can limit flexibility. So, if we take another look at the example above but change the management culture to one which is open, developmental, and progressive, we soon see the problem. As a result of my past experience I bring a patterned response of retroflecting which is unnecessary, inappropriate, and counterproductive. My colleagues interpret my behaviour as unnecessarily guarded and insufficiently open, and questions arise around my relational skill.

# Ways we interrupt contact, and consequences: Part 1

This and the next chapter explore what may be understood as defence mechanisms, or, in Gestalt language, interruptions to contact. These are best seen as patterns that have value and contain meaning whilst also having consequences for the quality of our connection with ourselves, others, and the environment. They include desensitisation, introjection, projection, retroflection, deflection, and confluence. I will briefly describe each. What is important to note is that they each connect and interrelate in complex ways, and I will illustrate this through case referencing.

## *Desensitisation*

Desensitisation is precisely that: being cut off from our senses. It refers to when we numb or block out sensation – physical, psychological, and emotional. As a protective mechanism, it's important for our well-being and survival that we have this capacity. We desensitise for good reasons – to reduce or avoid pain and discomfort, to keep from feeling flooded and overwhelmed with grief, to switch off from an experience that's unpleasant or unbearable. Busy managers and leaders with very fast-paced lives do it to just get through.

We do it when we travel on overcrowded subway trains, when we visit the dentist, or when we turn our ankle whilst walking in the mountains. In order for doctors and those in the emergency services to perform certain aspects of their jobs, at times it is important to be able to shut off from the reality of what they are doing. The job would be too disturbing and painful otherwise. More extreme examples include war, abuse, and a whole range of traumatic experiences.

In the business context, we may look to detach as a reaction to the exhaustion caused by incessant, fast-paced work schedules. Parents of young children may sometimes do the same after long periods of childcare without a break or insufficient support.

Coaches working with senior executives and busy managers often hear the story of getting through the week and using their weekends to decompress and re-energise sufficiently to start all over again. The consequences can be significant, as this coaching client spells out:

*At home, I often feel as if I'm only half there, they get what's left of me and I have a habit of retreating and opting out. I see time at home as recovery time from work. I really don't feel good about this but I don't seem to find a better way. I know I'm probably storing up trouble for the future ...*

The less healthy use of this interruption to contact is when the 'off' button is permanently switched off. It is now in automatic mode; it has become a pattern, a way of being. The individual is deep inside their fortress with the drawbridge up.

## *Introjection*

Introjection is a Gestalt term which refers to the process of 'swallowing' whole the beliefs, attitudes, values, and behaviours of significant others, especially authority figures. This happens most obviously in early life, and many of these introjections are useful, and even necessary. When children are about to put their fingers into an electrical power socket, or when they're about to run across a busy road, a simple 'No!' is what's required. This is not a consultative process; parents want this to be introjected. On the other hand, classic edicts such as 'never leave anything on your plate', 'know your place and don't try to get above your station in life', 'be strong', 'you can't have it all', 'big boys don't cry', etc., are all likely to have far more significant impact unless later in life they are brought into awareness and re-evaluated.

The negative consequences of introjection occur when internalised 'shoulds' and 'should-nots' or 'oughts' and 'ought-nots' prevent people from being able to seek and achieve satisfaction of important personal needs. Their internal rules get in the way. For example, the girl who grows up with the message 'you should always put others first' may well struggle to assert her own needs in adult life – or even know what her own needs are. When asked by her coach 'What is it you want from your life?' or 'Where do you want your career to go?', this individual may look perplexed and reply 'I really don't know. I don't often think about those kinds of things'. Another familiar theme runs something like this: 'I've always done work that others want me to do. I'm not sure if I've ever really chosen any role I've been in. They've been someone else's idea – their goals, not mine'.

A far-reaching implication of introjection is that we can never fully know how much of what we think and believe about the world is undigested material from our past.

From this perspective, an important aspect of developmental coaching is about discovering what we believe, what we want, and who we really want to be. As we proceed on this self-authoring journey we may still choose to hold on to much of what we have introjected, but from the knowledge that we have examined it and made it our own. Some stuff will be dispatched overboard as we come to recognise that it's holding us back. This can be a liberating experience as the weight of the rucksack lightens and new possibilities for one's life come into clearer focus.

## *Projection*

Projection is when we think we perceive something in others that we aren't yet able to acknowledge or fully own in ourselves. It may be a quality, personality trait, attitude, behaviour, or feeling. These can be both positive and less positive qualities and characteristics.

Some people acknowledge qualities such as high intelligence in others, yet cannot see their own smartness and continue to compare themselves unfavourably with those they perceive to be more intelligent. They may be critical of someone else's aggression or anger whilst denying those feelings in themselves.

To be on the receiving end of projection can feel good when the individual is projecting positive attributes that they do not own in themselves. However, it is likely to be a short-lived sense of well-being. In time, it's highly likely that the projection will take a sharp turn in the opposite direction: we're all familiar with the 'hero to zero' paradigm.

When the projection is negative, contact of any meaningful nature can be extremely difficult and conflictual. We tend to avoid people who have a strong negative projection towards us. At the cultural level, negative projections can be dangerous and ugly. Racism is projection at the cultural level, wherein fear, hate, and anger are projected onto another group.

# Ways we interrupt contact, and consequences: Part 2

## *Retroflection*

Retroflection means to turn inward upon oneself. We retroflect when we believe it would be unwise – dangerous, even – to speak or act out what we inwardly wish to say or do. We perceive that there is simply too little support and safety to do so. In the workplace people 'strategically' retroflect to protect their careers, or for political reasons, on such a regular basis that it can become the norm rather than the exception.

We learn to retroflect from an early age. Children learn within their families what thoughts and feelings are acceptable and can be expressed safely, and which are not. Getting it wrong can result in physical or psychological punishment, or both, so the young person learns to keep things to themselves. In families where feelings of any kind have been suppressed and where 'sensible', 'rational', 'logical' thinking is preferenced, it can be very difficult in later life for offspring of that family to understand, let alone express, their emotions.

This becomes ever more complex when we recognise how introjects and retroflects intertwine. 'Be happy, smile, and be cheerful' translates into 'I need to keep my angry feelings inside because they aren't acceptable'. Worse still, if a person introjects that angry feelings are 'bad', then it's a short step to punishing themselves when they have them.

Turning inward what would better be expressed outwardly can have serious effects on our health and well-being, and may diminish the quality of our relationships. Instead of being easy and comfortable in the another person's presence, we either minimise contact because it's too difficult, or we maintain a superficial connection.

Whilst retroflection clearly impacts at the individual and relationship levels, it can also have a critical impact on organisational performance. Those who have spent their careers in corporate life or who have coached and facilitated teams will know this. Individual members of teams are often caught up in a culture of retroflection, whereby people go through the motions of teamwork and collaboration but at a deeper, more significant level keep their thoughts, opinions, and feelings to themselves. They withhold their full energy and commitment. It is not uncommon for the group norm to be 'Turn up, but keep your head below the parapet and don't say anything your colleagues or the boss would disagree with'.

## *Deflection*

Deflection refers to the ways we turn away from or divert attention from a problem or issue. It can be an intentional choice or a habitual pattern that is outside awareness. When we deflect intentionally we usually want to avoid something or someone. We're proactively reducing the space for stronger, more direct engagement with a person because there is tension in that relationship or situation. We're using deflection to maintain a distance. This is sometimes the best we can do in the moment.

The most common ways we do that are through jokes, ignoring the point, changing the subject, generalising, and moving on before an issue has really been fully addressed. The 'yes, but …'. response is another common deflection, as are being diplomatic, using the logic of keeping things in perspective, playing things down, and trying to cool emotions when conflict resolution really needs more authentic engagement.

What does it feel like to be on the receiving end of deflective behaviour? Perhaps you might want to think for a moment about recent occasions when this characterised the contact you had with an individual or group of people. Perhaps you were making a point that got sidetracked, or got into a deeper conversation that didn't go where you hoped it would. You may have felt unheard, ignored, brushed off, or diminished by the experience. Being on the receiving end can feel frustrating, irritating, and disheartening. Deflective behaviours have powerful consequences for here-and-now contact and longer-term implications for authentic relationships if they become patterned and fixed. They can also prevent people getting to grips with issues and reduce the possibility of resolution.

We should recognise that there can be helpful intentions behind deflective behaviour. If a group situation has become very tense and uncomfortable, a clever quip can break the awkwardness and bring relief. It may not be the right time or place for a serious, deep discussion, so the deflective comment may serve a useful purpose in that moment.

## *Confluence*

Confluence is where our boundaries begin to merge and difference is minimised. In marriages and close partner relationships each individual, though often one in particular, submerges aspects of their individuality, their separateness, in favour of closeness and proximity to the other. Closeness, in the sense of connection and intimacy, is a healthy aspect of human relationships. However, a confluent dynamic is where two people have unconsciously become a 'we'. In other words, there is connection but without sufficient withdrawal back into separate, individual identities. Confluent couples sometimes wear the same clothes, purport to like all the same things, and share the same opinions on matters.

In organisational teams the equivalent is 'group-think', whereby difference of viewpoint is not validated, and indeed can be perceived as dangerous and threatening.

The attractiveness of the confluent state is most often and most clearly recognised in the early stages of a love affair, when both parties want to be with the other all the time and to shut out the rest of the world. Each partner's friends can be seen as a threat or competitor for their attention and affection.

# The Gestalt Cycle as an orienting framework for coaching practice

The Gestalt Cycle is an orienting framework for all forms of Gestalt-based practice including coaching. It is typically represented as a staged process (see Figure 14.1). However, this separation into stages can seem artificial because in the natural order of things figure formation is more of a continuous flow, following a wave-like rhythmic pattern. This representation is captured in Figure 14.2.

## *The sensation stage of the Cycle*

Current reality defines the *sensation* stage. In the coaching context, it's what's most important at the time to the client, such as an emerging need, a felt sense, or something that's disturbing their equilibrium. It can be an exciting new opportunity, a dilemma or difficult decision, a nagging voice inside that doesn't go away, a re-awakening of unfinished business, loss, or the fear of loss. It may be a short-lived issue that can be resolved quickly or a signal for deeper developmental work.

The psychological and emotional characteristics of this stage include:

- Excitement and anxiety aroused by new possibilities
- A sense of being stuck
- Tension, unease, frustration
- Anxiety, sadness, pain
- Anger, guilt, or shame
- Big questions (about self and life)

PART I: THEORY

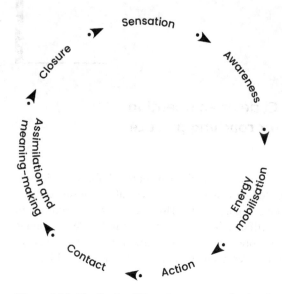

**Figure 14.1** The Cycle of Experience as an orienting framework

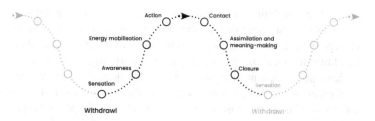

**Figure 14.2** The Cycle of Experience as orienting framework (wave representation)

## *Blockages and resistances*

At every stage of the cycle there are a number of ways we commonly defend ourselves from awareness. These interruptions (described in Chapters 12 and 13) are our protective mechanisms, some of which we're conscious of, some not. It's important to recognise the positive and negative impacts of these blockages and understand why we block awareness.

## *Common blockages at the sensation stage of the Cycle*

- Desensitisation: shutting down and cutting off awareness about something or someone
- Denial: not allowing ourselves to fully know or accept something
- Keeping the lid on our unfinished situations: suppressing and burying our thoughts and feelings
- Blocking our awareness of new possibilities: turning down opportunities, or simply not noticing opportunities that could meet important unmet needs
- Staying over-busy: keeping occupied in order to have something else fill our attention, time, and energy.
- Numbing out: for example, deadening our feelings through alcohol, drugs or social media

## *The awareness stage of the Cycle*

The *awareness* stage of the Cycle is about becoming curious, more reflective, and scanning both our exterior and interior worlds. It's characterised by going out to the world in search of data, ideas, and different ways of thinking and doing things, as well as looking inwards to better understand one's own internal experience.

The psychological and emotional characteristics of this stage include:

- Allowing yourself to really know what you want and need
- Discovering and articulating challenges and issues
- Deeper, authentic contact with self and personal truths
- New insights and the beginnings of a change in perspective
- Heightened awareness of choices and possible decisions to be made

- Greater sense of personal ownership and responsibility
- Embracing who you are – self acceptance

## Common blockages at the awareness stage of the Cycle

- Rushing ahead to problem solving before understanding enough about the critical issues and questions
- An urgency to move on and get to action rather than stay with the discomfort of not knowing
- Avoiding looking inwards and backing off from facing personal truths
- Keeping things secret
- Avoiding emotional connection with the issue(s) and people involved
- Withdrawal

## The energy mobilisation stage of the Cycle

The *energy mobilisation* stage of the Cycle is about moving from feeling stuck to becoming energised, from ambivalence to engagement. It's often characterised by an internal struggle between the forces driving and resisting change. Prior to a breakthrough there can be a sense of flatness and repetition, as if the client is going around the same story endlessly. This can produce a feeling of boredom in the coach or other listeners, resulting in a sense of frustration which literally transforms when the individual achieves a breakthrough.

Coaching someone who is profoundly stuck or staying within their comfort zone can test your capacity to stay patient and focused, especially for coaches with a strong bias towards action. You can find yourself losing interest and compassion, and your impatience can trigger unhelpful behaviours such as offering your solutions before the client is ready to find their own. However, when new insights emerge the wait usually feels worthwhile.

The psychological and emotional characteristics of this stage include:

- A freeing up of energy and motivation for action
- Movement: a shift or breakthrough
- Joining in, rather than staying outside on the periphery
- Recognising the possibility of meeting needs or achieving goals
- A sense of what needs to be done
- Coming up with new ideas
- Enthusiasm
- A readiness to commit

### Common blockages at the energy mobilisation stage

- Resignation
- Not engaging
- Backing off
- Staying outside or at a distance
- Going through the motions
- 'Managing' the coach, and the coaching process, to minimise impact

### The action stage of the Cycle

The *action* stage of the cycle is about translating heightened awareness into doing something that potentially changes the situation. It's characterised by learning, taking on new thinking and knowledge, changing behaviours, and growing new skill sets. It often involves taking risks and making a leap of faith to grow. In the coaching context, the focus on action is about exploring what can be done, how to do it, and when to do it. The coach supports the client to experiment, try things out, and learn by doing.

The *action* stage is not only about externally focused activity. It's also about internal experimentation and trying out different ways of meeting the world. For example, the exhausted executive with a strong sense of responsibility, and with an assumption that things go wrong when she doesn't take care of everything, might experiment with backing off, leaving a void, and seeing how else things might be resolved. In this case, her action would be *intentional inaction*.

The psychological and emotional characteristics of this stage include:

- Trying out new behaviours
- Having the difficult conversations
- Learning and practicing new skill sets
- Experimenting with new perspectives
- Holding old assumptions more lightly
- Showing up differently, re-inventing yourself
- Seeking out new ideas and thinking

### Common blockages at the action stage

- Failing to practice
- Stopping experimenting
- Failing to commit
- Failing to learn new skills or take on new thinking
- Procrastination – deferring action to another time

### The contact stage of the Cycle

Engagement, connection, and letting things in defines the *contact* stage of the Cycle. Being in stronger contact gives life a new vibrancy and we can feel more lively and energised. The world regains its brightness and colour. This more dynamic state can also be a time of anxiety as a consequence of showing up in a more open and vulnerable way. Holding old assumptions more lightly and changing behaviours don't come with guarantees of success. Leaps of faith are only such because there is no certainty.

The psychological and emotional characteristics of this stage include:

- A curiosity to learn
- A stronger emotional connection to yourself, others, and the environment
- Excitement and energy
- A sense of achievement, progress, getting somewhere
- Pleasure

## *Common blockages at the contact stage*

- Deflecting: not allowing something in
- Holding on to the old, not letting go
- Rushing to the next thing
- Undervaluing the achievement: 'anyone could have done it'
- Not banking: not taking in the positives from achievements, successes and near-misses

## *The assimilation and meaning-making stage of the Cycle*

The goal of Gestalt coaching is integration – a sense of personal coherence. If letting things sink in is characteristic of the contact phase, then the difference at the *assimilation* stage is that they have now sunk in. They are part of you. Things have come together in a new way and the world looks and feels different. Perspective has changed, 'reality' has changed, we have become a slightly different person. Your *ground* is reconfigured.

Whilst the very nature of change is that it's ongoing, and this stage will inevitably lead to the next, it's important to reflect, evaluate, reap the learning, take some satisfaction, and put a marker down.

The coaching conversation is about recognition of the challenges, struggles, ups and downs, and, most importantly, the ground that has been won – often hard-fought ground. It's a time of celebration.

The psychological and emotional characteristics of this stage include:

- Meaning-making
- Assimilation of learning
- Consolidation of change
- An increasing sense of personal coherence

## Common blockages at the assimilation and meaning-making stage of the Cycle

- Not taking the time and space to let the learning in
- Not letting go of the old; hanging onto something
- Fearing that closure means losing something or someone
- Fear of endings

# Part II

# PRACTICE

# Creating the conditions for deeper personal development and connection

## *Create the container*

The coach's first task is to create a strong enough container for the work. Developmental coaching, be that in the individual or group/workshop context, requires a holding environment that provides the protection, support, and psychological safety, as well as pressure and friction, to be able to engage in challenging inner work and relational contact. Creating the optimal *experiential* and *environmental* conditions that make for growth and development is an underestimated yet fundamentally important aspect of the coach's role. In terms of outcomes, it ranks as one of *the* most important critical success factors. So, what needs to be attended to here?

## *The holding space*

The venue must be suitable for the nature of the work. For individual coaching, this requires boundaries that provide safety, comfort, and confidentiality. Sometimes coaches don't pay enough attention to this and agree to coach executives in public arenas such as hotel reception areas or coffee shops, surrounded by people within sight and earshot. This inevitably puts limitations on what will and won't be addressed. If the client has some very difficult feelings around an issue, they are far more likely to bracket and contain rather than explore and express them – the holding space is not secure enough for in-depth work.

For team coaching workshops and other developmental group learning, the main conference room needs to be large enough, bright, and airy, with sufficient privacy. The seating arrangement should be informal, not boardroom style, there needs to be enough break-out rooms for small-group sessions, and sufficient time needs to be allocated. Time management in developmentally focused work is often a challenge, and it's common for less experienced coaches to underestimate the time required for self-exploration processes.

There also needs to be agreement around the use of technology during individual and team coaching sessions. The general rule is that laptops, mobile phones, and digital devices are switched off and put away (except during break times) in order that people can give their full attention to the process. The exceptions to this are when an emergency or on-call scenario means that someone has to remain available. Also, there are an increasing number of people who use their mobile devices to make notes to capture their thinking during sessions.

## *Hold the space*

Experienced practitioners expect to encounter anxiety in the client system at any point, but especially at the outset of new work. Helping people settle, and not being disturbed by the anxiety that can build in the client system, is part of the job.

When the work is underway we should remember that a significant part of the coach's role is to hold the space. This is most evident when there is a greater intensity and depth to the work and individuals begin to look to the coach for reassurance that all is well – or, at least, that it will be in time, if not right now. That reassurance comes from your presence, and the timing and skill of your interventions. The unspoken questions often on the minds of clients include 'Does this coach know what they're doing?' 'Do they know where we're going?' 'Do they have the skill and experience for this?'

Staying grounded, steady, focusing in the moment, and providing an attentive presence without rushing to premature action is often what's most required in testing moments, but we should not underestimate the challenge of that.

## *Build trust and create psychological safety*

So, starting from the positive and building from there is not simply a tactical matter – it's fundamental to the process of facilitating growth and change.

Simon (2009) makes the point that it is foundational to Gestalt theory that people grow and develop to the extent that they are open to new learning, and that requires a sense of trust and safety. He notes that whilst coaches may have expertise, experience, and knowledge that can be helpful to the client, a pre-condition for genuine learning is that the client be available, interested in, and engaged in the partnership for learning. He adds that the emphasis on trust is particularly important in organisational settings where evaluation of success or failure is an ongoing part of the client's everyday experience.

Whilst in principle there is a shared responsibility for establishing trust, in practice the onus lies more with the coach. With some clients this can take a long time, particularly if they have had negative experiences of professional helpers in the past or, more significantly, if their personal background contains experiences with primary caregivers that have left an enduring issue around trust. On the other hand, trust and connection can sometimes build surprisingly quickly and the client may be ready to get down to work.

For the client, trust enables them to feel safe enough to say whatever they need to say and to reflect on mistakes, failures, and regrets – to engage with the process of looking into themselves. For the coach, trust has several dimensions, but two are especially important. The first is to do with integrity, and the second, competence. Whether you are an external or internal coach, there will be times when you possess extremely sensitive and delicate information about individuals in an organisation. Sooner or later, for example, you will discover that someone is about to lose their job before they know it themselves.

You may become privy to plans for major restructures, mergers, and acquisitions. One careless, indiscreet comment can completely undermine trust and potentially wreck the coaching relationship.

Competence issues arise when clients experience coaches as questionable in their approach, judgement, or behaviour. Despite the fact that most coaches understand that their role is to facilitate rather than tell, some coaches can be prone to advice-giving and playing expert. The client who seems to be looking for answers may initially appreciate these pearls of wisdom. More experienced clients, who understand that coaching is essentially a facilitative, non-directive process, will be left wondering whether their coach really understands the true nature of the role.

# The relational stance and dialogic attitude

The relational stance and commitment to dialogue are as much about an attitude and philosophical position as they are methods or techniques. Gestalt practitioners seek to bring this way of being-in-the-world into every area of their lives, in contrast to being professional practices brought out at work and put away again later.

## The characteristics of the Gestalt coaching relationship

The Gestalt coach approaches work and life from the belief that there are some fundamentally important relational characteristics that need to be recognised and practiced. These are authenticity, respect, non-judgement, sensitivity, inclusion, confirmation, support, and courage. Together, they contribute to building connection and providing an environment of psychological safety and trust.

## Inclusion

This is the practice of wholeheartedly tuning into the experience of the other whilst retaining a strong sense of yourself and your own existence. It is an expanded version of empathy. The phenomenological method is the tool which supports Gestalt coaches to discover and understand the experience of the client. In this method, our own assumptions, judgements, and interpretations are bracketed. We are actively interested in discovering the cognitive, emotional, physiological, and spiritual experience of the client, as well as the meaning they make of their experience.

## Confirmation

Confirmation is similar to and more than acceptance. In confirmation, the coach recognises and acknowledges the client as they are right now. This does not necessarily mean agreeing with or liking what they are doing. Confirmation also includes the affirmation of the client's potential that they may realise in the future – aspects of them which are denied or alienated (Yontef 2002).

The Gestalt coaching approach encourages you to bring more of yourself to your work, share your thoughts, feelings, and your personal experience of being in the coaching relationship. It invites you to be open, connect more deeply, be moved, and, at times, say the difficult thing. It requires the courage to be fully present, not to hide behind the role of expert, to let go of the need for certainty and control, and, when necessary, to acknowledge your mistakes and regrets.

## Authenticity

From a Gestalt perspective, the coach needs to be authentic and creatively use their presence in service of the work. To be authentic means to bring more of yourself to your work – and not just the appealing, affable self. If we are too strongly invested in being liked by our clients, whether for psychological or commercial reasons, or both, we may suppress our edgy, dissonant selves in favour of keeping things pleasant and comfortable. Sometimes we need to tap into our rumblings and grumblings in order to dredge out an observation or reflection which may produce a difficult moment and yet also spark some rich learning.

When we are able to access more of our authentic selves and take the risk to go beyond where we've been before, we begin to fulfil our potential as a coach; this will show up in our level of awareness and our capacity for contact and connection. It's when you're operating at the boundary between what you thought you knew about yourself, and what you're actually capable of.

## *Be fully present in the moment*

This begins with being fully present in our work – and everywhere else for that matter. The mantra 'wherever you are, be there' captures it. We all recall times when we were 'in the chair' but not fully present. To be present means turning up as grounded and centred as you can be. Each of us has our own way of doing this and it may be as much about bracketing off our own issues as it is about tuning in to the other. Sports coaches go for a run, do some limbering up, and prepare themselves physically and mentally for their day. Gestalt coaches need to find their personal ways to achieve a state of focused attention where they are sufficiently energised for the work.

## *The dialogic attitude*

Engagement with dialogue can be seen as a technique or method, but from a Gestalt perspective it is seen as an approach to relationship and connection. The rationale is suggested in this quotation:

> *When people come together to practice dialogue ... the conversation gets progressively more authentic. People share the truth of their experience and listen to the experience of others. The deeper the conversation gets, the more the assumptions and beliefs that shape our collective reality have a chance of being exposed and re-examined. As these assumptions and beliefs are re-written, group behaviour can change.*
>
> *(Anderson 2011)*

Whilst the case can be made that everyday communication in both individual and group contexts is often a world apart from what's described here, it's also true that many people do have experiences of this kind – even if they're few and far between. And if they reflect on them, they often say that time seemed to take on a different feel, that it had a kind of magical quality about it – something happened that transcended 'normal' conversation and interaction. No one single individual took them there. It was more about the whole than the parts, and the whole became more than the sum of its parts.

During moments of dialogue, truths, assumptions, and projections emerge from behind the invisible curtain. They come into *the light*, and get recognised and examined afresh. Self-reflection takes on an extra dimension – the capacity to share thoughts and feelings, and simultaneously *observe* our thoughts and feelings *as they're arising*.

The capacity to create the conditions for, and then engage in, *dialogue* is a highly valued aspect of the Gestalt approach. *Dialogue* has to be co-created – something emerges that comes from both or all those engaged in the 'conversation'. It doesn't happen when someone is over-dominating, over-talking, under-listening, withholding, or claiming rightness. No one is sovereign in dialogue.

The process of sharing personal truths and perspectives in a spirit of inquiry and joint exploration can produce precious outcomes and a deeper sense of connection with self and others.

To enter dialogue is to risk change and, from a Gestalt perspective, this is a two-way street. The coach impacts the client, and vice versa. The potential exists for each to be touched, moved, and changed by a process of interaction that is controlled by neither but emerges out of connection, curiosity, and deeper engagement.

The capacity to be in dialogue with others is widely regarded as a *practice that expands perspective*, not least because it requires deeper listening, paying greater attention, balancing advocacy with inquiry, and more openness to learn from others. Guidelines for dialogue groups are presented in Chapter 21, which examines creative experimentation in group and team settings.

# Core principles in practice

## *Begin with what people are doing well*

Working with leaders and using feedback processes to identify core strengths and their flipside can be a powerful part of an executive coaching process. From a Gestalt perspective, interventions should be firmly grounded in the recognition of strengths before moving to less-developed competencies.

For some clients, it's difficult to take positive feedback onboard and they can be dismissive of it. Experienced coaches familiar with this challenge tap into their creativity to try to land the positives. Newer coaches need to find their own ways through this type of resistance, whereby the client insists on rushing on to the list of areas for improvement. Sometimes you can feel that you are fighting a losing battle and the best course of action is let it go and move on, suggesting that the individual reflects on the feedback at a later date and pays attention to the positives.

There are two primary reasons why it's important to start with what people are doing well. Firstly, many people don't fully appreciate what they have and who they are. They're simply not aware of what they do well and what they do best – it needs to be pointed out to them and this can be embarrassing for some so they want to get it over as quickly as possible. However, is protecting someone from temporary feelings of embarrassment a good enough reason to deprive them of important data about themselves? Secondly, personal growth and increased self-efficacy is a product of banking our achievements, successes, good attempts, and near misses.

## *See everyone and don't pick favourites*

When you're working with groups and teams it's usually the case that we see and connect with some individuals more than others; the consequence can be that some go unnoticed. These people may experience this phenomenon everywhere in their lives and have developed a creative adjustment to it. In some ways, it may suit them to be in the background and barely noticed – the focus of attention isn't on them. On occasions, we give these people less attention because they are harder for us to connect with or they trigger our own material, so we focus elsewhere.

If we've also picked favourites and are giving them unequal airtime and attention, it's highly likely that others will notice this and feel aggrieved, which will impact trust. And given that many people habitually compare themselves with others, they may come to the conclusion that the coach thinks their favoured ones are 'better than me' in some way.

Experienced practitioners often go out of their way to make contact with everyone in a group or team situation, sometimes in obvious ways such as shaking hands with everyone, ensuring they get everyone's name right, and giving everyone equal airtime. More discreetly, they are often to be found during coffee breaks having a quiet word with those who are not taking up prominent roles in group time. They may also proactively reach out and ensure that the people they themselves find most difficult to connect with are not lost in the shadows.

## *Look out for patterns – in individuals and relationships*

Sometimes, individual habits and behavioural patterns emerge quickly and become visible to the observant practitioner. Styles of relating – such as always going first or last in a group check-in, excessive banter or deflective behaviours, overt attention seeking, over- or under-talking, playing expert, or name-dropping – get noticed not only by the coach, but by others too.

When patterns are less obvious and visible, it's important to be patient and relaxed and just let them emerge. There are some signs that will alert you – for example, hearing something repeated several times or with a different energetic expression.

Noticing individual patterns and how clients characteristically show up and respond is a primary focus for the Gestalt coach. However, it should not be the exclusive focus. In any group context, it's equally important to notice and begin to recognise relational patterns and contact issues between people. This often requires the same level of patience and the discipline to resist rushing to conclusions and ungrounded action. Relational patterns come in many guises – here are just a few: behaviours associated with power and hierarchy, such as cosying up to the boss or hiding issues that might bring disapproval; who gets listened to and heard, and who doesn't; how leadership and influence occurs; who is in the light and who's in the dark.

In group and team coaching contexts, the Gestalt coach needs to be ever-mindful of viewing the field through both the individual and the relational lenses, and to be mindful of the key message of Field theory – namely, that we can only ever really understand another person when we take into account their context.

# Practitioner presence: The intentional use of self

Sometimes you might judge that a more evocative presence is required – a softer, calmer, more gentle presence intentionally geared towards building the necessary level of trust and safety for self-disclosure, risk-taking, and the expression of emotion. On another occasion you might sense that a more provocative presence is needed. In this case you may adopt a more challenging, confrontational style, choosing your words deliberately and expressing them more forcibly. This implies being able to bring a different presence to different contexts.

## What is meant by presence?

Some readers may be struggling with the concept of presence, associating it with charisma or style, which can be aspects of presence but only go part of the way towards defining it. From a Gestalt perspective, we all have a signature presence, whether we're aware of it or not, and it emanates from our distinctive way of being and acting in the world. Who we are, and how we present ourselves to others, is what determines our presence.

Our presence is a composite of many things: our physical characteristics and appearance, including age, body, size, posture, skin colour, dress choices, and hair-style; gender; sexuality; role, position, and status; values; voice, communication, and articulation; energy; creativity; spirituality; political and social beliefs; quality of self-awareness, capacity to listen, pay attention, and empathise; and general mood.

And it's our presence that contributes to whether we attract and interest others, and whether they find us convincing. As such, it's an important source of our capacity to influence. Equally, it can explain our lack of impact. Compelling presence typically comes from the authentic living out of who you are and what you're about. Conversely, when people experience a discrepancy between what an individual says they stand for and how they come across in their way of being in the world, their presence is inevitably weaker and less convincing.

Because the issue of our presence only becomes relevant and meaningful when we're in relationship to others, what we imagine our presence to be is far less important than getting rich feedback from others on how they actually experience it. Ideally, we need to hear from as wide a range of people as possible. Some might tell us that they like our humility because it comes across as unthreatening; others might refer to the same quality as being too quiet and 'invisible'.

Self-development programmes can provide the opportunity, in a structured way, to learn more about how others experience our presence. In our Courage and Spark vertical leadership development programme, we regularly include such a process. Our experience, however, is that people mainly share the positive aspects and tread very lightly on anything that might be received as negative. This is usually experienced as affirmative and confidence building – outcomes that should not be undervalued. Nonetheless, if we are to more fully understand the impact of our presence, we may have to proactively find ways to hear both sides of the story. This is why Siminovitch (2017), who has written widely on this subject, refers to understanding our signature presence as the domain of self-work and personal development. In contrast, she describes the use of self as the way we access our awareness and resources, to create interventions and outcomes that serve the client: 'Presence is the integrated totality of what we have developed and worked to become; use of self is how one leverages one's presence to impact and to strategically provoke client work'.

## The use of self: bringing greater intentionality to your presence

This implies being able to adapt your presence to different contexts and needs as you perceive them. And this presents the coach with two challenges: the first is to recognise what may be needed and make good judgement calls about how to use self in relation to that situation. Secondly, once you have a good sense of what's needed, you need to be able to follow through and provide it.

When you are considering what kind of presence to bring to a situation it can be helpful to ask yourself the question 'What is the presence that is lacking or absent in this situation?' You might then choose to bring that presence as an intentional way of influencing and effecting change.

A final point about the intentional use of presence: you might think that it's only when you *do something* that you exert influence and impact a situation. Whilst this is part of the story, it's also the case that your very presence, your *being*, can change things.

## The challenges of intentionally using self

Casement (1985) was one of the first to make the separation between *the observing self* and the *experiencing self* – referring to our ability to look objectively at our thoughts, feelings, and behaviours as well as experience them from the inside. Kegan's (1994) 'subject–object' theory speaks to a similar theme. Things that are in *subject* are experienced as unquestioned, simply a part of the self, such as an assumption about the world or a pattern of behaviour. They are taken for granted because they *are* our reality. *Object*, on the other hand, means that we can see something, consider it, re-evaluate it, and potentially act on it and change it.

Self-development work enables us to develop our *observing self* and expand what is in *object*. This is important because the Gestalt approach requires a developing capacity to reflect on your own experiencing, what you observe and sense in the other, and in the relationship between you. And to do all three whilst the work is happening.

These capacities enable the coach to use self as an instrument of influence through tapping into their own experience of being with the client and using internal data selectively as a source of intervention.

## *Developing the use of self*

It's important to remember the purpose of using self as an instrument: to heighten awareness, provide feedback on impact, and bring attention to characteristic patterns of behaviour and group interaction.

The use of self requires an ability to assess what your inner radar screen tells you, and to differentiate between your 'own material' and the 'client's material'. Therefore, the more you understand about your own long-standing, deep-rooted patterns and assumptions about the world, the better placed you are to use yourself safely and effectively as an instrument of change, confident that you are acting with sufficient self-awareness. Without this, you may always feel anxious about bringing too much of yourself into the equation and potentially hijacking the client's agenda.

So, how can you know what belongs to you, what belongs to the other, and what has arisen out of co-creation? For certain, the coach who has engaged in little self-examination may lack the self-awareness to discriminate between their own and their client's issues. Projection is not something that only operates in one direction – client to coach. All coaches get triggered from time to time and are then more prone to project onto their client. These are the moments of unsteadiness when coaches can make questionable comments or interventions that are off the mark. This is why it is essential that those who work psychologically and incorporate the use of self into their working approach subject themselves to deeper processes of regular supervision and ongoing personal development, preferably in both one–one and group situations.

As stated elsewhere (Bluckert 2006), *the personal development of the coach is every bit as important as theory and skill development* and, really, there is no meaningful distinction between the two. The implications for coach development generally, and for those who intend to work from a Gestalt approach in particular, is that professional training programmes need to incorporate a strong focus on awareness development and deeper self-exploration.

# Creative experimentation and improvisation

Early Gestalt practitioners incorporated creative experimentation and improvisation into Gestalt therapy, and it has been a hallmark of all forms of Gestalt practice ever since. In this section of the book I present three interconnected chapters, beginning with an outline of what's meant by experimentation in Gestalt, followed by a chapter on individually focused experiments and another focused on experimentation in group and team contexts.

The Gestalt coach has what Zinker (1994) called 'the permission to be creative'.

Experiments are one of Gestalt's core methods for expanding awareness through experiential discovery. Several types or forms of experiment are associated with the Gestalt approach, including enactments, exaggerations, and reversal. In the examples that follow it will become clearer how these can feature in experiments that centre around the better-known 'chairwork' method.

## *The 'chairwork' method*

Experienced Gestalt practitioners may argue that chairwork has been used so often it can't really be described as an experiment any more; instead, it's become a tried and tested technique. Nonetheless, the empty chair process is always a step into the unknown and holds the spaciousness for fresh improvisation. Chairwork experiments are never identical, and there are always points of decision and the element of unpredictability.

One of the reasons why it's used so frequently is that it works well with several different issues. It can be used to expand awareness of relational issues, inner conflicts, disowned parts of oneself, and interruptions to contact such as projection. The empty chair can represent someone else, the organisation the individual works for, different aspects of a dilemma, or a life decision.

## Case example

One of the most common issues brought to business coaching is the situation where a coaching client describes a relationship difficulty they're having with their boss or another colleague. As they tell the story they can be surprised at the strength of feelings they have. At a certain point you might ask the client 'And have you said any of this to the actual person'? More often than not, the reply is 'Well, not in the way I've just told you. In fact, I've kept most of it to myself'.

Experiments arising out of this common scenario can take the form of try-out behaviours within the boundaries of the coaching conversation and/or outside of it. Inside the coaching conversation you might suggest that your client metaphorically 'brings the person into the room' and speaks directly, in the present tense, to their boss/colleague. The construction of the experiment could be something like this:

The coach presents their idea to the client and invites them to participate in the experiment. If accepted, the coach brings in an empty chair and positions it, with guidance from the client as to how near or far away it should be. The invitation from the coach then might be 'So, just imagine Sally is here right now. What do you have to say to her?' (enactment). This is likely to feel strange in the early stages, and it may take a little while to get going. Once the client tries this out and begins to find what they want to say, you might notice that they are very subdued in their way of expressing it – despite saying that they feel strongly conflicted. You might suggest that they try speaking with more force and energy to see what happens then (exaggeration). In turn, this could produce a stronger contact with the past event and enable a breakthrough or emotional release.

This kind of safe expression within the boundaries of a coaching conversation can be sufficient to produce a sense of resolution and closure around an issue. On other occasions there might need to be a real-life conversation with the boss or colleague. The experiment in the coaching conversation then functions as a rehearsal, or try-out, for that.

## *Working with polarities and different parts of ourselves*

One of the ways the chairwork process has been used since the early days, when Fritz Perls used it in his classic topdog–underdog experiments, has been to uncover the nature and power of polarities and give voice to different parts of ourselves.

Two or more chairs are set up for the client to experience, and then speak out from, different parts of themselves. Examples of these include:

- The highly self-critical self in dialogue with the kinder, more self-compassionate self
- The individual who recognises a habitual way of responding to the world which is acquiescent speaking to the self that feels angry about being taken for granted
- The person who see brilliance and smartness in everyone other than themselves, and projects outwards what they are not seeing and owning within
- The individual who feels she has to present as cheerful, optimistic, and happy everywhere in her life in dialogue with her sad and worried self
- The dutiful, over-responsible self in dialogue with the self that just wants more me-time and to find the playful, fun-loving, happy self

## *Practice considerations*

Working in an experimental way provides coaches with infinite opportunities to be creative and inventive. It begins with the coach suggesting a brief pause in the coaching dialogue to test interest in the client for an experiment that the coach has in mind. The client will not always understand what is being offered here and may need a clear explanation in addition to the invitation. The idea proposed by the coach is merely the starting point for the experiment. Once underway, the coach has to monitor whether the experiment is becoming productive. You may need to alter the direction of the experiment if it isn't engaging the client or seems to have gone up a blind alley. You also need to be conscious of grading your interventions in line with what the client can cope with and appears ready for.

The experiment might take the client, and the coach, to the deep end of the swimming pool too quickly – before they have accessed sufficient self-support to stay there – in which case they will probably look to you for that external support. Maybe it feels too strange and alien, or it provokes shame and anxiety.

On the other hand, they may be looking to you because they feel stuck and want some help to get moving. They want to go deeper but don't know how and are requesting a gentle push.

For the coach, it's important to keep in mind the intention for the experiment, be ever mindful of grading, not get lost in the drama, and not let the process become formulaic.

These and other considerations show how the practice of creative experimentation is a craft, and one which requires supervised practice to acquire mastery.

Here are some guidelines for good practice:

- An experiment should emerge out of the context, the story, the dialogue, and real, felt experience
- It should be sufficiently challenging as to offer the prospect of new learning, but not so much so that the client is overwhelmed with anxiety, embarrassment, or shame. The capacity to

responsibly grade experiments is as important as the level of creativity within it
- No matter how much care and attention you pay to grading an experiment, people can quickly find themselves in strong contact with their internal reality. It's not unusual for them to be surprised by the strength of feelings they have about something or someone. Emotional expression is therefore to be expected when working in this way
- Experiments should take the form of an invitation to try something. You need to give careful attention to explaining the intention of the experiment and what you're hoping it will achieve
- Agreement should be sought first and the experiment, where possible, should be created in collaboration
- Experiments can raise resistance so you need to be attuned to when a client is meeting their barriers. Taking steps around or reversing from a hurdle can be more appropriate than encouraging someone to leap over it
- There are always choice points in an experiment. These include staying with it or letting it go, bringing more elements of the situation into play, and suggesting active techniques such as exaggeration, enactment, and reversal
- Timing is important: any intervention can seem absolutely right and yet fail to land due to misjudged timing around openness and receptiveness
- Experienced Gestalt practitioners seem to make creative experimentation look easy, but it's not. It's a craft that takes time and practice to achieve excellence. It also requires the courage to take risks
- We need to keep in mind the broader objective of encouraging an experimental attitude or mindset

### *Figure and ground*

Experiments typically form out of current figures, as outlined in the case examples. The experiment provides a vehicle for externalising what has previously been internalised, and the expression can be cathartic and produce breakthroughs. We may see the value of experiments as helping people to achieve some resolution around today's figures. But it also goes beyond this. Mann (2010) captures this well when he says

*An experiment that facilitates the expression of anger at an authority figure can lead to a reconfiguration of the client's field in relation to his expressing strong emotion. Such a change occurs in the ground as new embedded awareness sediments down, replacing past creative adjustments.*

# Individually focused Gestalt experiments

Angela, a finance director of a media organisation, received feedback that she needed to think about the nature of her day–day interactions with colleagues and the quality of relationships. It was couched like this:

*Your work is fine, in fact it's excellent. However, I sometimes feel, and I think your colleagues see it similarly, that we don't really get all of you. And it leaves a question mark over your authenticity. The reason why this is important is it affects your relationships and, more importantly, maybe there's something we could be getting that we aren't'.*

She and the rest of her colleagues in the executive team were about to embark on a facilitated team coaching process which included a 360-feedback process, so she saw this as an opportunity to test whether her bosses' comments were replicated by her peers. They were, and she made the decision to discuss the report with her executive coach:

*A recurring theme is that I keep myself to myself too much. My peers and the CEO don't feel that they know me despite having worked together for more than three years. I'm not surprised to receive this message – it's been intentional behaviour on my part. Though I now see how this is negatively impacting the quality of my key relationships. I've made a decision to change this, but need to explore how.*

In a coaching session, she considered some ideas and made a commitment to try out some new behaviours. These included regularly initiating conversations, ensuring her one–one meeting with the CEO happened at least monthly, and making social arrangements with colleagues. She also committed to contributing more in executive meetings on the whole agenda, rather than confining her contributions to her functional area only. Significantly, she decided to take the risk of letting her colleagues know why she had been so careful about sharing her opinions earlier. She told them that she had suffered a major loss of self-confidence and esteem in the previous leadership team and had felt bullied and intimidated. She had experienced high levels of anxiety and feared that if she were to express her views, they would be dismissed. Worse still, she would be seen as underpowered to operate in an executive leadership role.

Angela's big experiment was to risk being herself and to have the courage to express her views. This could have confirmed her worst fears that she would be judged badly, which could lead, ultimately, to her losing her job. As it turned out, it had precisely the opposite effect. The CEO was more reassured when he felt he was in connection with the whole person, and her colleagues welcomed the more relational, contactful Angela. Gradually, she regained her self-confidence as well as the respect of the team. When she reported her personal insights in a subsequent coaching session, here is what she said:

> *What I came to see was that my previous strategy of hiding myself could have a worse consequence than taking the risk to show myself. By showing myself I risked losing my job – and I definitely didn't want that. But by not showing myself, I risked losing myself.*

Marcel, a CEO of a Swiss healthcare organisation, put it this way:

> *I used to think that a good CEO should never share how he was feeling about things with staff in case it caused uncertainty and doubt. It could lead to people having less confidence in you. Now I see it completely differently, so I've been experimenting with sharing more with staff, and not just with my own team. I have 'CEO Get-Together Time' with groups of staff at more junior levels and I'm far more authentic with them now. They don't want me to give a packaged story so I trust that they can handle more*

*of how it really is. I'm having conversations about how we want to work and live – what kind of purpose we have together. These are developmental conversations, not just about task or results. And I can tell you, they love it, and so do I.*

## Other experiments arising out of coaching conversations

It's not uncommon for clients to recognise the life experiments they wish to try out following some sharpening of awareness. One client created this question for himself, which he resolved to make into an ongoing life experiment: "Can I come at life and work in a different way – an easier way. That's my experiment?"

Another senior leader framed his question, and experiment, like this:

*I've been leading an organisation that achieves its objectives from anxiety. I see it everywhere. And here's the painful truth. It comes from me and my anxiety. I'm committed to change that, and my experiment is to continue to lead a successful company but one where people are no longer fearful and worried – I want them to come to work and leave it, happy and feeling good.*

## Readiness to deal with unfinished business

Finally, this executive made a significant personal commitment to work on some difficult personal issues after many years of grappling with the question of whether to try to keep the lid on, or take the step to get some help with it. His reflections afterwards were:

*Getting on with this sooner would have been better but I know I wasn't ready. Already things are changing. I have committed to reinvesting in my family and friends and so as a result I plan my personal diary ahead of my work diary. This is my experiment and it's a first for me.*

# Experiments in group and team contexts

## *Contact in the group or workshop context*

When you begin work with a group or team, one of the first things you notice as you walk into the room is the way it's been set up. In Chapter 15, I covered the importance of creating the optimum holding space for Gestalt work, whether that's with individual coaching clients or groups and teams.

The layout of the room, whether people are seated around a main table or a circle of comfortable chairs, and the proximity between people all have an influence on contact. In team coaching workshops or Gestalt-based leadership development programmes I (or my team) typically arrange the chairs in a circle, mindful that whilst the intention is to encourage conditions conducive for open sharing, this can be experienced as intimidating to some people who would prefer to sit behind a table. The chairs are therefore arranged at what seems like a 'safe distance': not too far away, but not too close either.

It's interesting to notice how some people move their chairs in or out to suit their own preference, but mostly the circumference of the circle remains pretty much the same from the beginning to the end of the day unless break-out conversations in pairs and triads disrupt the pattern.

To bring this to people's attention and encourage a spirit of experimentation, we often invite the group to explore what contact and connection might feel like if we were to change the proximity or distance we are sitting from one another. The experiment typically follows this sequence of graded experiments:

Step 1: keeping the circle intact, move all your seats to the furthest point back towards the walls (in a large room people are usually about 5–6 metres away from each other at this stage). Now, and without words, notice your felt experience – what you're experiencing in your body, your breathing, what you're feeling and thinking. Take another moment to consider the possibilities for connection and contact at this place.

After about a minute…

Step 2: now move your chairs in by around 1 metre. The same instructions apply again – notice your felt experience, etc.…

After about a minute…

Step 3: now move in with your chairs another metre. The same instructions apply again – notice your felt experience …

After about a minute…

Steps 4 and 5: the same as above, by which time the group will be very close. Depending on the room size, there may be one final move in, until people are literally as close as possible.

After about a minute (which can seem a very long time for some people), the process is reversed…

Step 6: move back 1 metre and notice your felt experience…

And then just keep moving your chair until it's where you feel right – not as a group, but as individuals.

Now notice your felt experience and notice where the configuration has settled.

End and review.

This is a contact exercise during which people often experience what is known in Gestalt as the contact boundary. They know it because it is a felt experience in their bodies – maybe their breathing changes, for example. It is like an invisible line that they come up to, and step through and beyond. It can feel temporarily uncomfortable, yet at the same time intriguing.

Their awareness is raised about where their personal contact boundary is and where fellow group members meet theirs. The exercise also raises awareness of what the possibilities, as well as limitations, are at different places and boundaries.

The outcomes of this exercise vary in relation to the timing of when it's done and the experience the group has of intimacy work. With groups of fellow practitioners who have worked together for a long period of time, they may want an enhanced level of connection from the beginning of a meeting and will quickly self-organise to achieve it. Groups and teams who have yet to establish closer intimate connection may be reluctant to engage with this sort of exercise, at least until there is more preparation of the ground.

Invariably, when done at the 'right' time for a group, it can be a pleasing experience and one that they want to repeat. Most often, the group finds a place of proximity which is noticeably closer than the original configuration.

## *Experimenting with dialogue groups in team coaching*

Practicing dialogue is an experiment in itself, and the desire to be in dialogue requires an experimental attitude.

During a leadership team coaching assignment, one of the most obvious features was that they were most energised when discussing new business opportunities and reviewing financial performance and commercial results. These topics had a magnetic effect on them and drew them in. Given that they were the executive team running a major company, this was no surprise.

I had introduced them to the notion of strategic/intimate (described in Chapter 6), and they saw themselves operating almost exclusively in the strategic and paying insufficient attention to the intimate. They recognised that they needed to find more of a balance. When I asked them to give their first thoughts on how they might do this, they said they should find time and ways to have conversations as a team which were not about problem-solving or arriving at an end result.

I proposed that they experiment with being in a group dialogue session for one hour using a number of guidelines that would probably steer them *away* from a results-focused conversation. They agreed, and I introduced them to the following guidelines. I would remain out of the circle and after an hour we would review the experience.

### Dialogue group guidelines

- No group-level decisions will be made in the conversation
- Suspend judgement in the conversation
- As you suspend judgement you are simultaneously as honest and transparent as possible
- Try to build on other individuals' contributions in the conversation
- Make 'I' statements, as opposed to speaking for the group or for anyone else in the group
- Be present in the here-and-now experience in the room

At the outset of the session it was hardly a surprise to find that they were uncomfortable, puzzled, and somewhat awkward. They had a tried and tested way of being together and this wasn't it. They didn't know what to focus on because there was no set agenda and no topic. They started conversations and then stopped them because they quickly recognised they were falling back into finding a problem and solving it. They regularly referred back to the guidelines but it took around half the session for them to find a new groove. They started to experiment with sharing more about themselves and what they were experiencing in the here and now. The engagement level steadily increased and they visibly relaxed. By the end of the hour they were in contact with each other in a way I had not seen on any of the three previous team workshops. When I called time, they asked for more because they were enjoying it so much.

In the review that followed, these are some of the things they said:

- 'Wow, what a freedom that gave. I just felt freed up by not having to come up with a plan, a solution, a to-do list'
- 'I felt I could go anywhere – actually I felt quite emotional at times – and it made me realise that I normally only bring my brain to these meetings'

- 'There was a different connection starting to happen here – and I for one really enjoyed it'
- 'Yes, we shared more of ourselves and it didn't seem to matter that we weren't on an agenda looking for a result. In fact it was a breath of fresh air'
- 'Well, you know, there was a result but it was a different kind of result. It was the intimacy result we talked about. I think we seem closer right now, and more relaxed. Imagine if all our meetings felt like this?'
- 'We should do this more often and not just on team off-sites. How can we bring this back? It brings something completely different into play. Communication is so much better and less formulaic'

Readers who would like more on the guidelines may be familiar with David Bohm's four key principles of dialogue, which are the first four on the above list. The additional two come from Gestalt group-work practice.

# The unit of work as a team learning experiment

## *The unit of work concept*

One of the primary reasons people don't always integrate learning is that they fail to complete units of work. Instead, the compulsion to rush on to the next task without paying sufficient attention to reflection takes over. Teaching people how to complete units of work plays an important role in the process of efficient meaning-making and banking of experience.

The value of the unit of work is that it provides a notional boundary around open issues and themes, in contrast to the familiar scenario where new issues are raised but nothing is given enough attention to achieve resolution and closure.

The unit of work concept developed by members of the Cleveland Gestalt Institute was devised to show a process of opening (beginning), dialoguing (middle), and ending (closing out) on themes and issues before moving on to the next – thus making the process more effective, functional, and satisfying.

## *Case vignette*

At the first workshop of a team coaching process one of the directors described the situation of the company in these dramatic terms: 'If we don't transform this company then it'll become extinct. We'll be remembered as the team who turned the lights off. It's really as simple as that. Disagree with me if you think I'm wrong or exaggerating our position'. Nobody did.

So, with the gravity of the occasion starkly expressed, there was an urgency to get on with serious discussion about what to do. In fact, this was not the first time the team had created some protected time to address its urgent business challenge. They had organised a number of Away Days to get to the core issues, with the expectation that they would go on to agree a new strategy and plan of action. These had been chaired by the managing director and had been useful in surfacing the unpalatable truths, but also frustrating because there was little else to show for the investment of time and energy. Divergent perspectives on the core issues had been expressed, revealing little common ground regarding solutions.

As I began to take in the group interaction in the opening session I observed that each of the eight executives was eager to advocate their own view of the problems, yet with little connection to the previous speaker's contribution and certainly no build on it. Within a few minutes there were as many items for attention as there were individuals in the room. They then vied with one another to get further airtime on their own preferred 'figure', and through force of argument some succeeded in getting a response from others. The number of open, unresolved issues swiftly grew from eight to twelve to fifteen. Nothing was worked through or closed. The emotion and energy in the room varied from intense frustration to complete switch-off. The MD and HR director looked anxiously in my direction as if to say 'get us out of this!'

## *A small experiment*

I chose to let it run a little longer before asking 'On a scale of one to ten, ten high, what figure would you give for the quality of content discussion right now? And what figure would you give for the group process and interaction?'

The content discussion scored higher than the quality of group process and interaction. I then asked them to find one word to describe how they were feeling. Six out of the eight came up with exactly the same word: 'frustrated'. One said he'd metaphorically left the room twenty minutes earlier, and the other said he was just biding his time for the mayhem to subside and then he'd enter the dialogue. Later, he described the communication in the team as 'soul-destroying'.

In my experience, this leadership team story is not particularly unusual, and I have witnessed similar well-intentioned groups of successful individuals with good instincts and ideas struggling to collaborate effectively. The group pattern of opening up multiple issues and failing to stay with any of them through to closure is familiar to those in corporate life – this despite the resulting frustrations that characterise so many leadership team meetings and which explain why they can be such fraught and tense environments.

In essence, this team needs to learn something it hasn't yet mastered. From a Gestalt perspective, they could benefit from learning to complete units of work and then maintain a level of team discipline around it. Carter (2008) describes the unit of work as having four steps: 1) assessing 'what is'; 2) choosing what to attend to; 3) acting on the choice; and 4) closing out the activity. This simple process links well with the Gestalt Cycle around awareness raising, energy mobilisation, action, gaining closure around issues, and the assimilation of learning arising from the experience. Here is how it worked through with the group communication problem identified in the case vignette above.

## *The bigger experiment*

Having shared my observation about their communication process with the team, I discussed with them the notion of the unit of work and suggested we engage in an experiment with the purpose of learning more about how they might improve their interaction and in turn reduce their frustration with one another and their process. They cautiously accepted the invitation.

We began by reasserting the 'what is' regarding their tendency to open up several themes and issues, leave them out there without closure, and the resultant frustrations. They were clear that they wanted to break the pattern. Team members identified several aspects to the problem: a tendency to advocate rather than listen and inquire, a belief that theirs was the 'right' solution, anxiety to find the solution because so much was at stake, and a consultative leader with a very tolerant style not given to call time with people. The more they focused on the 'what is', the more they gravitated to the view that group facilitation was not a strength in the team so they often lost the process and communication would get chaotic. They agreed what to attend to first: improving the facilitation of group dialogue.

The experiment they created was to use the remainder of the day rotating the facilitation of each session. One person would take the role up to lunch, followed by a different team member in the afternoon. The rest of the team would offer feedback to these volunteers and there would be an overall review of the quality of group dialogue at the close of the day.

A very different energy and emotional climate soon replaced the previous one. The team quickly re-engaged with the content with a heightened level of awareness around behaviours and group interaction. Each volunteer team facilitator did a good enough job, received some constructive feedback, and became more aware of the challenges of occupying that role with the team. The usual occupier, the MD, got a break from it, was able to participate more fully in the dialogue, and was re-assured to hear the volunteers acknowledging how hard it was. The pattern was highlighted, interrupted, and altered. More importantly, the team began an important learning process around how to complete units of work.

# Structured awareness-raising processes in Gestalt coaching

## *Verbal 360-feedback*

From a coaching perspective, the purpose of the feedback process is to gain outside perspective from a wide range of stakeholders. Most managers and executives have been subject to at least one 360-feedback exercise in their careers, so the practice is usually well understood. More often than not, an online questionnaire will have been used, so this may have set the expectation for how 360-feedback is done. However, my own preference is to use a verbal feedback method that involves conversations with a range of people from the client's work context and their wider life. Normally I recommend speaking with around fifteen people, including the individual's line manager, a number of peers and direct reports, some additional internal colleagues, external customers, family members, and friends.

When clients first hear about this method, it can be something of a surprise and tends to produce a mixture of excitement and apprehension. They quickly see the difference between 360 processes they've done in the past using an online questionnaire and the approach they've just heard about. Questions arise about whether they will involve family and friends, and, if so, who. At this point guidance needs to be given around seeking permission from those people to engage in a confidential conversation usually conducted by phone or video call.

The semi-structured conversation, lasting up to an hour, can be focused around the following themes, or variations thereof:

**111**

1  What is X doing well?
2  What are their most well-developed strengths and what do these bring to the organisation?
3  Are any of these overused or overdone? If so, what can be the consequences?
4  What is it like to be on the receiving end of X? What is her/his general impact?
5  What areas for improvement and development stand out to you?
6  If X were to be one shade braver in his/her life, what would you wish for him/her?
7  What's the 'one big thing' you'd most like X to commit to?
8  Miscellaneous – a catch-all for anything not fitting into the above.

The presentation of the feedback is through a written report that contains the anonymised verbatim comments with no interpretation or analysis added. It's presented purely as the 'what is'. Any meaning-making is left to the face-to-face coaching session when the report is discussed in detail.

The volume of feedback produced by a verbal 360 process can be considerable, and there is inevitably duplication of comments and repetition of issues. In the preparation of the report, care is therefore taken to only reproduce distinct comments and issues rather than every single comment. Even so, the report can run to several pages, which means that there is a lot for the coaching client to take in. For this reason, I schedule up to half a day for this meeting.

A cautionary note: this may not be something every client wishes to sign up for. There can be reservations, particularly about who will ultimately see the report. Also, some clients are sensitive about being the subject of yet another exercise where they feel they are being assessed, judged, or pigeon-holed. Ensuring that the client fully understands the process, its purpose, and the potential benefits is therefore essential; even so, on some occasions they will refuse it.

## *Lifeline sharing – making the connections and seeing the patterns*

Coaches have their own ways to take the personal history of their clients. Some do it through conversation, and others through structured exercises. My own preference is to use the lifeline exercise. Here is a brief description.

The instructions to the client are:

*On the flipchart sheet, draw a long line, straight or curved. On the far left, write the year you were born. Put an arrow pointing back to the past. On the far right, note today's date and finish the line with an arrow pointing to the future. On your lifeline, include: family background, education, career, the birth of siblings or your children, the death of a loved one, and the beginnings or endings of important relationships. Include times you can now see you were in transition. Also cover personal high and low points, achievements of which you are proud, and events you have regret about. Think about the people who have had an influence on your life, even if you never met them but only knew about them. Briefly describe them and the impact they had on you. You may have experienced numerous relocations due to parents being in the armed forces. You may have had more extreme experiences such as civil unrest or family trauma. How have these events affected you? Include both personal and professional events. Review your emotional journey and include times when you felt happiest and most engaged with your life, as well as those times when you felt stuck, lost, sad, or confused. Pay attention to the emotions you feel now as you remember and write these things down.*

The value of the lifeline for the client is that the act of reviewing one's life through a structured, in-depth process of this kind connects them to their felt experience and sheds light on what has shaped the person they are. It often reveals a sense of continuity and meaning. A less obvious benefit is that it helps people to remember what they'd forgotten and this can be an important part of the awakening process.

For the coach, the benefit is that you gain a deep perspective about your client's life and their *ground* – the bedrock of their experience. At later points in the coaching, this becomes invaluable in making sense of how today's issues and challenges have their echoes from the past.

For the client, the lifeline process can heighten awareness of some important themes and issues. These are a small selection from recent sessions:

- 'Career has always dominated my life to the detriment of my marriage and family life – in truth I've neglected them'
- 'Others have always made the important decisions regarding my career progression. I've just gone along with it'
- 'It's clear to me that I make hard work out of life and I want to live easier'
- 'I see now that I've spent my life running someone else's race'

# Support, challenge, and dealing with complexity

## *Support*

The commonly accepted definition of support used by Gestalt practitioners is 'that which enables', and it includes both self-support and environmental support, which, in the coaching context, can come from the care, attention, and empathy shown by the coach. As a coach, it's important to recognise that clients vary in how they let support in, or even *whether* they can let support in. This creates an important challenge for any coach, which is to find *that which enables* for different clients.

Sometimes the most supportive thing you can do as a coach is to listen attentively whilst your client offloads. These are times when clients are so overloaded that they just want to get it all out, squeezing out the sponge that is now too full. Developmental coaching in these circumstances is often not possible. Your client is just too exhausted and frazzled.

But we should not underestimate the supportive impact of feeling understood and affirmed by another human being. Experienced coaches will be able to recall moments of connection with a client when both you and they experience a felt sense for the deeper meaning and importance behind the words. And, more than this, your client can see your felt sense, it's evident to them. You may be very moved and become tearful yourself, and just for a few fleeting moments you truly know one another: contact.

## Challenge

We should also recognise that senior leaders often say they want a high level of challenge from their coach and begin with an expectation that they will get this through regular, thought-provoking questions and observations and a certain amount of respectful provocation.

Some coaches will choose to go a step beyond this level of challenge and take the view that a more confronting presence is required in certain circumstances. The call they make is often based in a sense that milder forms of challenge haven't achieved much and it's time to move the dial up. This is likely to be a higher risk intervention, and some coaches will not necessarily feel competent or comfortable in doing this. They may also have a philosophical difficulty with a more confrontational approach. The reasons for moving the dial up are to deepen the work, enhance contact in the moment, and facilitate a breakthrough. Most experienced coaches, when they look back on their work over the years, will recall moments when they've chosen to take a more challenging approach. Whether it always worked is a different issue, but it's likely that they will say that in some instances it proved to be a pivotal moment in the coaching and transformed their relationship with their client for the better.

Achieving the fine balance between support and challenge is one of the most important factors in building effective coaching relationships and, at the same time, one of the most difficult things to achieve. As a coach, it can therefore be helpful to receive feedback on how your supportive and challenging interventions are being received by your clients.

## The challenge of increasing complexity

In organisational leadership contexts, clients are regularly challenged by the increasingly complex nature of their roles and from working in fast-paced, results-oriented environments. And they are invariably trying to do this without sufficient support, and with an internal operating system that has got them so far but may be overheating in its attempt to deal with a very different level of challenge. If complexity exceeds capacity, the inevitable consequence is that it can leave clients feeling stuck, in over their head, worried, and doubting their ability to come through on the right side. They can then fall back on old, outdated, and patterned ways of dealing with the world that don't produce what's needed. The classic ones are to work harder and work longer, getting more and more tired whilst also knowing deep down it's not enough. Sadly, this is an increasingly common story in organisational life – and beyond – as expressed by this senior leader:

*I used to find one level of complexity a challenge but grew the muscle required to deal with it. Then it became two and three levels and I struggled more and more to keep up. Now there are just so many moving parts. It's enough just trying to get my head around each of them but the real challenge now is that most of them are interconnected and sometimes I feel as if my brain is frying'.*

## *Vertical leadership development*

So, what is the role of the coach in these types of circumstances? As a foundation, it's important that the coach provides a strong holding space to ensure sufficient psychological safety to face the challenges inherent in their 'what is' – their current reality and their experience of it.

Beyond that, the best way to support *and* challenge these clients may be to signpost them towards specific processes that can accelerate their development. It's therefore important that executive coaches working with senior leaders, along with practitioners working in social and political contexts, acquire a strong theoretical and practical background in leading-edge, vertical leadership development. This is important because support and challenge will not always be enough. It is part of the organisational coach's role to help their clients develop the transformational capacities and perspectives expected in leaders, such as personal maturity, bigger-picture systemic thinking, visioning, transformational route-mapping, creating developmentally organisational cultures, a dialogic attitude, an experimental mindset, a more evolved understanding of resistance to change, and the capacity to influence effectively. Some of the skill sets associated with these are outlined in Chapter 26, 'Resourcing the client'. Others are outside the scope of this book and are covered in detail in my mini-book *A Comprehensive Guide to Vertical Development* (Bluckert 2019).

# Gestalt-based vertical leadership development programmes

Up to this point, my primary focus has been on the Gestalt approach within individual coaching and with teams. In this chapter I discuss the use of the Gestalt coaching approach within vertical development leadership programmes – a newer and less known way in which Gestalt principles, theory, and practice are being applied to assist leaders with their growth and development within ever more challenging and complex organisational environments.

These programmes are primarily individual development interventions; however, when an organisation commissions such a programme to be delivered to a critical mass, or even all of its senior leadership population, the benefits can be felt at the wider system level. In other words, the programmes become an organisation development intervention as well, impacting the leadership culture and beyond.

## *Horizontal learning and vertical development*

Recent interest in horizontal and vertical development has brought to people's attention that most leadership development processes, and learning in general, has been based on the premise that if we equip people with knowledge, skills, abilities, and behaviours, then those will later translate into improved competency and performance. This paradigm is a technical one, wherein problems can be broken down, analysed, and fixed so long as we have acquired the necessary technical knowledge to deal with them.

An analogy frequently used to describe horizontal learning is the act of pouring water into a glass. As more knowledge, skills, and competencies are acquired, the glass fills up. When deficits are identified, the answer is to add new or better ones into the glass. People who search for new tools, techniques, and models are effectively on the same mission: to fill their glass. From this perspective, excellence in management and leadership – or, for that matter, in any form of practice – is achieved by filling the glass with the best possible content available.

In contrast, the purpose of vertical development is to expand an individual's ability to handle complexity and 'sense make' in ambiguous and uncertain situations. The analogy here is to increase the glass size or leader's worldview.

The process of vertical development involves inner change, psychological breakthroughs, and emotional contact, and it is not always visible to the untrained eye. Sometimes it's only months or years later that people notice and say 'there's something different about you now'.

Cognitive understanding of vertical development can be a useful starting point and may create a shift of consciousness. However, on its own it's unlikely to be enough. The journey of vertical development is primarily an experiential one, and this is where Gestalt-based holistic development programmes can play an important part.

## *Gestalt vertical leadership development programmes*

It's still the case that most leadership development programmes are heavily steeped in the horizontal learning method, wherein delegates are provided input on leadership theory, case studies, competency-based skills frameworks, and models of explanation, delivered primarily through lectures, PowerPoint presentations, and small-group discussions. The very language used to describe these programmes reflects their conventional nature: classroom learning, training courses, leadership seminars. Energisers and experiential exercises are often part of the mix to break things up, but the overriding approach is outside-in, informational learning, delivered by scholars, consultants, trainers, and facilitators expert in the leadership development field.

Vertically oriented leadership programmes are still fewer on the ground despite the fact that there have been versions of these running in many parts of the world for far longer than the vertical development concept has been around. Experiential programmes designed to raise self-awareness and enhance interpersonal skills in managers were first introduced in the mid-1940s, using methods that would still be new and progressive to many people today.

Contemporary versions of these experiential programmes have kept this tradition alive and pushed at some of the same frontiers encountered by the original Gestalt pioneers. One such programme, Courage and Spark©, designed and delivered by the author and the Courage and Spark faculty, is an example of this. An immersive, five-day residential workshop, Courage and Spark© uses a Gestalt approach to accelerate vertical development in both senior leaders and next-generation high-potentials.

## *The value of Gestalt vertical leadership programmes at the individual level*

- They can act as triggers for psychological and emotional development because they tend to be uplift experiences where people make significant personal breakthroughs. For some, it may be their first experience of deeper self-exploration in a group context.
- They provide the skilled help, experiential conditions of high trust, psychological safety, non-judgement, and support that enables transformative growth.
- They can be a safe enough place where there is sufficient support and trust to share one's truth at a deeper level, opening up and feeling the feelings.

- They can be an important reflective space where individuals uncover what they have been formerly subject to, such as core beliefs and assumptions.
- They can provide that precious experience of being seen, heard, and understood.
- They can help individuals see how they may have turned against themselves, and the cost of that for them. Also, they may help them draw a line under that and instead commit to finding a sense of peace and self-acceptance.

Programmes of this kind are usually experienced as intensive, powerful, and memorable events. It's not unusual for people to refer to them as life-changing, and to say that *they've come back to themselves*. The sense of shared experience and community is equally important to many people – 'the sense of belonging to something greater', as people often describe it.

Organisations that sponsor such programmes are mindful of what happens next and, post-workshop, seek to support their people through a variety of means. These include conversations with line managers, internal coaching, selected use of external coaches, and therapy where appropriate. All parties tend to be acutely aware that the precious learning and development emerging from the programme can get lost when people re-enter their normal, busy, demanding schedules and wider lives.

### *The impact on leadership culture of Gestalt vertical leadership programmes*

Some organisations that sponsor vertical development programmes seek to support learning beyond the individual level. They are curious to see what difference this kind of experience can have at different levels of the system, such as team and organisation culture.

What they find is that the tight, supportive group experience, where deep connections were forged, carries back and impacts the organisational leadership space – sometimes in a transformative way. The Gestalt approach also provides a template of what aware-contact and healthy intimate connection looks and feels like, and they want to cascade it to their own teams.

# Resourcing the client: Relational know-how for dialogue and effective collaboration

## *Developing interpersonal capacity*

The relational skills set out in this chapter enhance social, psychological, and emotional capacities, which can transform the quality of relational connection and group interaction. In essence, they are about how to talk, listen, and become curious and interested in one another – a set of competencies it might seem that everyone possesses. However, life experiences regularly remind us that they aren't always well developed and the need for enhanced relational know-how in all spheres of life remains an urgent priority. And when they're insufficiently developed, it presents real obstacles to what is possible in terms of dialogue, group co-operation, conflict management, problem solving, and healthy, close, intimate relationships.

Whether we're looking at teams in business or non-commercial organisations, social and political collaboration in the wider community, or our primary relationships at home, the interpersonal capacities described here are critical to effective communication, achievement of desired outcomes, motivation, and wellbeing.

Many Gestalt coaches regard the teaching of relational skill sets as an important part of their role. This 'teaching' can happen within the one–one coaching context, in team workshops, and in leadership development programmes.

## *Quality of attention*

I begin here because it's so fundamentally important to be on the receiving end of quality attention, and, when it happens, it can feel like a gift. And this raises the obvious question: why isn't this happening more often in my life?

Time constraints aside, for many people this is not a well-developed competency and, additionally, paying quality attention to others requires conscious effort. The quality of the attention any of us can provide depends on the shape we're in – physically, psychologically, and emotionally. If you're exhausted, distracted, stressed, or emotionally triggered, this inevitably affects the quality of attention you are able or want to offer.

Giving good attention starts with giving rather than waiting and involves listening well, getting curious, and actively inquiring into the other person's world and their experience – not in a transactional way or in service of an agenda, nor as a means to an end, but as an end in itself. When people experience someone really paying attention to them, the nature of their contact with themselves, and with you, changes. It's as if they wake up and come alive, and the possibilities for deeper connection suddenly expand.

This practice of providing quality attention demands that we become more available and proactively reach out. And when people experience unexpected interest and kindness, they feel seen, recognised, and affirmed.

## *Listen to understand, not to advise or fix*

A common form of listening is *listening for*, in contrast to *listening to*. *Listening for* typically serves the purpose of getting enough of the other person's story to move in with your own advice, solutions, and perspective. In fact, it's such a common form of listening and style of relating that we hardly notice it, especially if that's what we tend to do ourselves. We may also believe that it's what people want and expect.

*Listening to* is an altogether different thing. This is about really hearing someone and taking the trouble to understand their meaning-making and tune in to their construction of the world.

## Ask different kinds of questions

For some people, first base is to *simply ask more questions* and get more interested in the other without seeking to bring the conversation back to themselves or fading out.

They may have a habit of sharing their own opinions and experience too quickly, or for too long, and fail to reciprocate sustained interest in the other. Whilst people generally give extra allowance for these behaviours if the individual is in crisis and is atypically preoccupied with their own needs and issues, it's not a great basis for mutually satisfying communication in the normal run of things. It can put a drain on the relationship bank and can be interpreted as a lack of self-awareness and emotional intelligence.

The new muscle to be built here is to ask more and different kinds of questions – and to sustain attention for longer. Going about our everyday lives, we sometimes hear someone asking a different kind of question and it stops us in our tracks and makes us think.

So, the challenge is to discover what makes a powerful, impactful, beautiful question and regularly experiment with putting them out there. Finding great questions can be the key to both strategic and intimate conversations. A good question is immediately relevant, a catalyst for new thinking and meaning-making.

## Share your own thinking and commit to understanding others' perspectives

The process of growth and maturation as a human being invites us to grapple with, and sometimes incorporate, different perspectives so that our own worldview becomes larger, more comprehensive, more nuanced, and more sophisticated. This is challenging because it means suspending our own views and beliefs, and being open to new ways of seeing, understanding, and making sense of the world.

Allowing greater flexibility between protecting your known self and identity (who you are and have been) and allowing new things in, which might change you, is at the heart of personal growth and development.

The significance of this for the coach is the challenge to stay with the tension between supporting the way the individual currently configures their experience, makes meaning, and meets the world, and supporting the energy for difference, novelty, and change.

### *Notice the quality of the contact you're in with yourself and others*

Regularly check-in with yourself and deepen your appreciation of what you're in touch with. Notice how present you are – and where you go to in yourself. How alive do you feel? Or, conversely, how shut down, flat, or withdrawn do you feel?

Get more curious about the impact others are having on you and hearing the impact you're having on others. Ask yourself 'What's it like to be on the receiving end of me?' If the answer is that you don't really know, see whether you're ready to find out, and, if you are, seek out feedback from people who will have something useful to say to you and who are well intentioned.

If your tendency is to reflect on your inner world *after the event*, and then later try to process what just happened, you are not alone: many people do this. However, when you have the capacity to reflect in the moment, and to see what's happening, it gives you more leverage to change your behaviour and be more impactful. This is what was meant earlier about being aware of your own awareness.

# Practice guidelines for the Gestalt coach: Part 1

It's time to join up the principles, concepts, perspectives, and activities presented in the earlier chapters and build a set of practical guidelines for the Gestalt coach. The breadth of content requires two chapters.

## *Attend to the story and content whilst remaining attuned to process*

Coaches need to understand their client's challenges and issues in order to appreciate their world and how they see and experience it. So, the client's story is important. At the same time, it's important to retain a process perspective, and this can be difficult when serious matters are being shared which may have significant implications for the individual, their team, and the organisation as a whole. The urgency and anxiety present in these scenarios can unsettle coaches and tempt them into trying to come up with bright ideas to help solve the problems.

Nonetheless, as a Gestalt coach your primary contribution is in the process space, and that requires highly developed observational skills to take in patterns of interaction and the quality of awareness and contact. New problems and challenges will always emerge for your clients. Your role is to help the individual, group, or team become better equipped to deal with them.

## *Track issues and bring unfinished material back to the client's attention*

In coaching conversations, issues and themes emerge and recede until something stands out more clearly, usually with greater energy around it. A stronger emotional connection often accompanies this, and the focus of attention may need to remain there for some considerable time, during which you can easily lose track of previous figures (items of interest or concern).

When you see a master practitioner at work, you'll probably notice that very little seems to get lost. They have the ability to focus on the prominent issue of the moment (the figure), whilst also keeping tabs on a number of topics raised earlier that didn't get attention. Some may not matter because things have moved on and the issue has resolved itself through another discussion. Others may need to be brought back to achieve closure. This is especially important in group situations because individuals can perceive that their issues have been relegated and received less priority than those of others. If this happens to them regularly, it can lead to a sense of being a less important member. In turn, it can produce a feeling of resignation and reinforce a tendency to withdraw.

## *Attune to your clients' characteristic ways of responding and their contact patterns*

At the beginning of a concert I recently attended, which featured an exceptional guitar soloist, the audience had to wait longer than usual for the musician to get started. The musician gently told the audience he just needed to take his time to 'settle' before beginning his first song. And he took quite some time. Eventually he began, and the audience got what they were hoping for. The reason I tell this story is that I was struck by hearing someone who knew precisely what he needed in that moment, and this was him responding to the situation in a way that was right for him.

I've told this story to several people. The reactions have been interesting. Most have said something like 'You know, I never do that. I don't settle myself. Not even sure how I'd go about it. I just get on with it'. After some self-reflection, another person said, 'Well, I know how I typically respond. As soon as anyone puts an idea to me, I always start with "No". Maybe later I'll back track but my habit, my pattern is to start with no'.

Everyone has their unique ways of being-in-the world and their characteristic ways of responding to life situations. Returning to the coaching context, it's therefore part of the coach's remit to develop an appreciation of how their clients typically meet the world – how they self-organise and manage their lives and relationships. Do they move towards, away from, or against people and situations? Are new challenges welcomed or avoided? Do they build up problems and cause themselves stress and anxiety? Do they scare or soothe themselves, play things up or play things down? What's their style of contact: up close and intimate whenever possible, dipping in and out, or staying at the margin to minimise the discomfort of intimacy? Do they quickly get angry, panicked, or stressed, or do they take things serenely in their stride? What are their patterns around support: overly independent and reliant on self-support, or more open to being helped?

All of these and more will surface and replay in the coaching relationship and, by making themselves visible in the here-and-now of the coaching conversation, also provide opportunities to explore and understand better.

## *Hone your observational skills and share what you notice in a clear, impactful, and non-judgemental manner*

Given that a significant part of the coach's job is to see and notice, what is it that we should be paying attention to? Firstly, we will notice things *within* individuals: their habits and patterns of thinking and behaving, their energy (or lack of), their ways of being and responding to the world, their styles of relating, and so on. Secondly, and this is especially true when we're working with groups and teams, we will notice things *between* people – relational dynamics. One of the defining differences between the novice and the more experienced practitioner will emerge in what they see, what they notice, and the difference can be considerable. This may be explained by the greater importance the experienced coach gives to staying longer at the awareness-raising stage rather than moving to interpretation or action.

Noticing what's happening in your client and in yourself is one thing; articulating it with impact is another. To do that, it's useful to keep the following in mind:

- Say things in a clear and understandable way, avoiding technical jargon and terms.
- Be economical with words. If the client is straining to understand you because it's lengthy and complex, it can dilute the impact.
- Offer your observations in a non-critical, supportive manner and without too much investment in whether they are *right*. Sometimes you will hit the mark and the client will immediately recognise and value what you have to say; on other occasions your offering doesn't make a great deal of sense to them, in which case you simply need to back off gracefully.
- Stay as close as possible to descriptive feedback rather than interpretation.
- Good articulation of inner data can take the form of metaphors or images. Experimenting with one's creativity is an important feature of Gestalt work.
- It's important to be bold and take risks. Nothing ventured, nothing gained.

# Practice guidelines for the Gestalt coach: Part 2

## *Cultivate 'context sensitivity' both in the immediate and wider field*

*Keenly observe what's in the immediate field (in the client, in yourself, and your relationship with one another)*

This requires a good eye, a keen ear, the capacity to tune into your client's sensory world, and the ability to pick up on contact issues between you. At the same time, a Gestalt coach tunes into their own *interior* world and notices what they're sensing, thinking, and feeling so as to be able to draw on that data to intentionally use their self as instrument.

The Gestalt coach will be particularly attuned to:

- The quality of dialogue
- The quality of engagement and level of energy
- The quality of awareness and contact
- The emotional climate

In a group or team situation the Gestalt coach will aim to tune into the individuals in the room, the relational dynamics between them, and how the system as a whole is functioning.

*Seek to grasp what's in the wider field, the client's context, and to assess how it may be impacting the present situation*

Clients exist within multiple levels of system, including intrapersonal, interpersonal, team, and organisation systems.

Corporate restructuring processes provide a clear example of how systemic forces may be acting on individuals and groups. Team coaches working with corporate leadership teams often become aware of decisions yet to be announced at the next level of system, the group level, which will inevitably impact individual members of that team. It's not unusual for only a minority of the team to be aware of this whilst the rest try to second-guess the scenarios. In this situation, the system is most definitely in the room, albeit in the shadows. The expression 'the elephant in the room' is often a reference to systemic issues that are currently in the undiscussable category.

### *Stay with direct experience and intense emotional situations without seeking to shut down the client*

The opportunity to ventilate feelings in a safe, holding space can be enormously important, particularly for clients who typically bottle things up, have nowhere else to express them, or who find themselves in a crisis situation. Nonetheless, they may be surprised or taken aback by the strength of feeling they have about an issue.

However, as I've written elsewhere, 'the role of the coach is not to go "hunting" emotions. Allowing and supporting the discharge of feelings when they naturally arise is all that may be necessary or appropriate' (Bluckert 2006).

Nonetheless, this can be a challenge for some coaches, as expressed in a very honest way by this coach when she revealed in a supervision session:

> *I'm OK with anger and frustration probably because they are the feelings I'm most able to express. But when it comes to hurt, sadness and grief I withdraw into myself and then try to move them away. It's because I don't allow these feelings in myself.*

This recognition was the catalyst for her to commit to some very important personal development, which benefited not only her professional work, but also her personal life.

## *Tune in with empathy and compassion*

This is a key enabler of connection and contact. It's more than listening carefully and becoming aware. It requires the coach to actively engage with the other person's world as they see it, so you can grasp their experience – and they know and feel it. They experience that someone is working to understand them. And it's more than just hearing their story and imagining yourself in their shoes. Something then needs to be conveyed, and usually it needs to come as much from the heart as from the head.

## *Help people learn how to complete units of work, assimilate learning, and make meaning*

This relates to getting closure around issues and attending to the withdrawal phase of the Gestalt Cycle. Whilst traditional coaching emphasises practical action plans and to-do lists as proper take-aways of coaching conversations, from a Gestalt perspective these are not always appropriate or relevant. Whilst there may be some back-in-the-world action to be taken, the outcome of Gestalt coaching is often an interior reconfiguration of self – a new way of seeing, perceiving, and feeling. The original issue can seem far less important and not require action.

An important aspect of the coach's role is to help clients make meaning and achieve new learning, and by attending to the final stage of the Cycle of Experience – the assimilation stage – the coach facilitates the completion of units of work. This is also the place where people can bank the positives from an experience, feel pleasure, pride, and satisfaction, or, in circumstances where things have not gone well, learn from failure.

It's important to note that this is also the stage of the Cycle where there is a withdrawal of energy and interest from the previous figure. This can be followed by a void before a new figure emerges or the coaching encounter draws to a close. Allowing a natural cycle to close out without prematurely rushing to the next thing is a hallmark of the more experienced, sensitive practitioner.

# Watch-outs for Gestalt coaches

## *Work creatively with 'resistance' without resorting to personal defensiveness or unaware advocacy*

By now it will be obvious that your purpose is not to take someone somewhere. Indeed, if you try to do that you will most likely increase the resistance that already exists. Your client will be resisting *you*. From a Gestalt perspective change is difficult, and we should anticipate that people often feel uneasy and ambivalent about it. Whilst they may glimpse the potential benefits, the fear of engaging and the perceived costs and losses may be more figural to them. They may simply be too fearful at the present time, or just not ready. And circumstances change: one day in the future, the very same individual who was walking away from their change agenda turns around and walks right back towards it.

In a very practical sense, this also makes the coach's work easier. You don't need to find ways to push through resistance. Instead, recognise and validate resistance as a form of creative adaptation. Without this capacity, people would be open to being manipulated and exploited in all areas of their lives.

## *Learn to recognise when you're triggered – and what to do about it*

There will always be times when we fall back and regress. Something or someone triggers us. We get restimulated by our unfinished business, perhaps over-react, perhaps project something onto someone else from a part of ourselves that we have as yet not fully owned. Irrespective of how committed we are to working on ourselves, we cannot expect to rise above everything. Despite the fact that our bedrock (ground) changes as we grow and develop, it will always contain the material that can hook us in the present.

We are especially prone when we're over-working and exhausted, ill, stressed, going through difficult times, or experiencing loss. These things knock us off balance. Disappointing as it feels at the time, it doesn't mean we've permanently regressed. We're probably just revisiting some old places.

## *Resist over-structuring, and hold models, concepts, and interpretations lightly when work is in progress*

There can be a temptation to turn to your toolkit of models, frameworks, and techniques – horizontal knowledge and information – to alleviate the anxiety and confusion that can surface when working in a more emergent, less structured manner. And sometimes, as a coach your anxiety, which may not be obvious to you in the moment, can take you into the relative safety of 'expert' and you find yourself downloading your latest favourite theory. Everyone has done this at some point, especially in the earlier stages of coach maturity.

Nonetheless, the capacity to offer theory-free responsiveness in the moment is essential to the Gestalt approach. Whilst there is a place for teaching, as already discussed in Chapter 27, the general rule in Gestalt work is to be economic on concepts and tread lightly here. The consequences of over-theorising show up in the quality of contact: the client may well switch off, or creatively adapt to you by showing interest in order not to be seen as ungrateful for your well-intentioned offerings. In effect, you have inadvertently interrupted contact.

In contrast, when you speak out in the moment your authentic response, person to person, about how you're impacted by hearing the clients story, the result can be a closer, more intimate connection and the precious experience of shared humanity.

## *Know your intention, and have a good sense of timing in your interventions*

As with any kind of intervention, whether it is high or low on skill and elegance, intentionality is always an important element. If the coach's interventions are made with a good heart and from considered thought, it's more likely to be well received.

A good sense of timing can make all the difference between an effective intervention and one that goes nowhere. Whether your client is an individual or a group, the challenge for the coach is the same: picking the right moment to intervene and making a contribution that is seen as valuable and on the mark. There are a number of considerations that inform decisions around timing. The first is to have a keen appreciation for where your client is right now. How open are they to what you're proposing or saying to them? If the individual hasn't finished telling their story they may not be ready to receive your reaction. They may still be feeling raw and vulnerable following some difficult news, significant self-disclosure, or tough feedback. Holding back and providing attentive listening can be wiser than making comments that don't land.

And, sometimes, the helping relationship is not sufficiently established for certain types of exchange. The issues here are around trust, rapport, and connection. Your client may not be ready to let you influence them – they are still wary, watchful, and need to keep you at a safe distance. Whether you're coaching at the individual, team, or organisational levels of system, the question of readiness for work should be in your mind: what can realistically be achieved right now, and has sufficient preparation of the ground been done?

# The training and development of Gestalt coaches

One of the challenges many coaches encounter with the Gestalt approach is how long it takes to get from an elementary, basic understanding to a deeper level of familiarity with its core concepts and genuine proficiency in its methodology and practice. If you recognise this yourself, you will probably resonate with Hanafin (2004) when he says 'I understood Gestalt for ten years before I realised I didn't understand Gestalt'. There are no easy answers here, no clever short-cuts: it takes time, discipline, practice, and regular access to skilled teachers and practitioners.

## Gestalt-specific training

Developing psychological-mindedness and making an ongoing commitment to working on your own personal development agenda provide the foundation for developing as a Gestalt coach. The next question is whether the Gestalt coaching skill set can be mastered without engaging in some kind of Gestalt-specific training. My own view is that whilst some of the guiding principles and values will accord with coaches from other traditions, it's improbable that a coach can truly work in a Gestalt way without some theoretical and practical grounding.

## Gestalt development programmes in consulting and coaching

The growing interest in Gestalt in organisational contexts has spawned several training programmes in Gestalt organisational consulting, from basic level introductions to advanced post-graduate degrees. Some of the leaders of these programmes in the UK, such as Paul Barber, John Leary-Joyce, Bill Critchley, and myself, have gone on to develop Masters-level business and executive coaching programmes based around or integrating a Gestalt approach and methodology.

Other similar programmes have emerged in Eurasia, Asia Pacific, and the Nordic and Baltic states, in addition to the coaching programmes offered by a number of US Gestalt institutes. The result is that there is now the opportunity to take a specific Gestalt-oriented coaching programme in many parts of the world. I will reference some of these at the end of the book.

## Recurring theme

You may have noticed a recurring theme throughout this book, and indeed all my writing about coaching, concerning the importance of the self-development of the coach. One of the central messages of this book is that whilst Gestalt principles, concepts, and practices are essential to coaching competency, the coach's journey of personal development is at least as important. This view has been held by seasoned practitioners since the beginning of professional coaching and was expressed well by Jaques and Cason (1994) when they wrote:

> *Coaching ultimately depends, for its effectiveness…on the level of adult development (maturity) of its practitioners. No 'experience' or 'expertise' can make up for the resources a more highly self-developed coach possesses compared to a less self-developed one. If we distinguish between what a person IS and HAS, the*

*latter can be suspended, or left unused. Only the former cannot be withheld and is therefore what really counts.*

## The importance of personal development

There are many routes you can take as a coach to deepen your personal development and gain greater self-awareness, insight, and personal mastery. Whilst it's beyond the scope of this book to provide a full and comprehensive inventory, I will offer a small selection of processes that I believe support the growth and development of coaches intending to work from a Gestalt-based approach.

## Working with a Gestalt coach

The issue of being coached raises an interesting point. Many practicing coaches appear to have little personal experience of being coached themselves unless they have undertaken training which incorporated the practice/feedback model of learning, or where a course requirement stipulated a certain number of hours of being coached. Working as the client of an experienced, skilled Gestalt coach can be an excellent way of absorbing the approach whilst at the same time doing your self-work.

## Working with a Gestalt supervisor

Similarly, it can be helpful if your coaching supervisor has a primary or secondary professional background in Gestalt. Some of the practices outlined here, such as creative experimentation and the intentional use of self, are not necessarily well known to all supervisors. Nor are some of the guiding principles and orienting models, such as the Field perspective and the Cycle of Experience.

## *Experiential workshops, ongoing personal growth groups, and communities of practice*

Attending personal growth workshops or becoming a member of an ongoing experiential group are also powerful self-development routes. These are feedback-rich group environments that offer a context where coaches can sharpen their awareness, experience a different quality of relational contact, experiment with new behaviours, and discover more about their impact and presence.

In these environments people learn about how they are seen, or even whether they are seen, and are supported to open up to themselves and others. In the process, many skills relevant to a Gestalt coach are tried out and fine-tuned, such as staying here-and-now focused, empathic attunement, and dialogue. The ability to give feedback in a skilled way is also learnt, as is the capacity to receive feedback in a less defensive manner.

People also learn more about being in groups and the important art of how to influence as well as be influenced. These are places where you can practice asking different kinds of questions, share your own thinking, and grapple with incorporating other's perspectives.

For those who have been members of ongoing groups (and there are some that have been in existence for many years), this becomes a special place where relationships of great depth and connection grow. For some people, these groups have been a central part of their self-development and an important source of learning for their professional development.

## *Personal study/reading*

Any list of methods to develop oneself must include reading and private study. There is now a substantial body of coaching literature, some excellent Gestalt publications, as well as an ever-growing number of self-development manuals that can open people up to new and inspirational concepts. As part of a wider range of development activities these make an important contribution. Reading the best literature and assimilating new learning will assist cognitive understanding and may expand consciousness, but in isolation will be an insufficient medium to develop the distinctive Gestalt skill set.

# References

Allan, J., & Whybrow, A. (2007). Gestalt Coaching. In S. Palmer & A. Whybrow (Eds.), *Handbook of Coaching Psychology*. London and New York: Routledge.

Anderson, R. (2011). *The Spirit of Leadership*. The Leadership Circle.

Beisser, A.R. (1970). The Paradoxical Theory of Change. In J. Fagan & I.L Shepherd (Eds.), *Gestalt Therapy Now* (pp. 77–80). New York: Harper and Row.

Bluckert, P. (2006). *Psychological Dimensions of Executive Coaching*. London: Open University Press.

Bluckert, P. (2014). The Gestalt Approach to Coaching. In E. Cox. T. Bachkirova & D. Clutterbuck (Eds.), *The Complete Handbook of Coaching*. London: Sage.

Bluckert, P. (2015). *Gestalt Coaching: Right Here, Right Now*. London: Open University Press.

Bluckert, P. (2019a). *A Comprehensive Guide to Vertical Development*. Peter Bluckert.

Bluckert, P. (2019b). *Vertical Development in the Workplace*. Peter Bluckert.

Carter, J. (2008). Gestalt Organisation & Systems Development and OD – A Past, Present and Future Perspective. *OD Practitioner*, *40*(4).

Casement, P. (1985). *On Learning from the Patient*. Hove: Brunner-Routledge.

Chidiac, M. (2018). *Relational Organisational Gestalt*. London: Routledge.

Critchley, B. & Stuelten, H. (2008). *Consulting from a Complexity Perspective*. Unpublished.

Gendlin, E. (1998). *Focusing*. Morton Walker: Everest House.

Hall, C.S., & Lindzey, G. (1957). *Theories of Personality*. New York: John Wiley and Sons.

Hanafin, J. (2004). Rules of Thumb for Awareness Agents. *OD Practitioner*, *36*(4): 24–28.

Hycner, R., & Jacobs, L. (1995). *The Healing Relationship in Gestalt Therapy*. Highland: Gestalt Journal Press.

# REFERENCES

Jaques, E., & Cason, K. (1994). *Human Capability: A Study of Individual Potential and its Application*. Falls Church, VA: Cason Hall & Co Publishers.

Kegan, R. (1994). *In Over Our Heads: The Mental Demands of Modern Life*. Boston: Harvard University Press.

Kegan, R., & Lahey, L.L. (2016). *An Everyone Culture: Becoming a Deliberately Developmental Organization*. Boston: Harvard Business Review Press.

Laloux, F. (2014). *Reinventing Organisations*. London: Nelson Parker.

Leary-Joyce, J. (2014). *The Fertile Void – Gestalt Coaching at Work*. London: AOEC Press.

Lewin, K. (1952). *Field Theory in Social Science*. London: Tavistock.

Mann, D. (2010). *Gestalt Therapy 100 Key Points and Techniques*. London: Routledge.

Melnick, J., & Nevis, E.C. (2009). *Mending the World: Social Healing Interventions by Gestalt Practitioners Worldwide*. Wellfleet: Gestalt International Study Center Press.

Melnick, J., & Nevis, S.M. (2018). *The Evolution of the Cape Cod Model*. Wellfleet: Gestalt International Study Center Press.

Nevis, E.C. (1987). *Organizational Consulting: A Gestalt Approach*. New York: Gestalt Institute of Cleveland and Gardner Press.

Nevis, E. (1997). Gestalt Therapy and Organisation Development: A Historical Perspective, 1930–1996. *Gestalt Review*, *1*(2): 110–130.

Nevis, S., Backman, S., & Nevis, E. (2003). Connecting Strategic and Intimate Interactions: The Need for Balance. *Gestalt Review*, *7*(2): 134–146.

Nevis, E.C., Melnick, J., & Nevis, S.M. (2008). Organizational Change through Powerful Micro-Level Interventions. New York: *OD Practitioner*, *40*(3): 4–8.

Parlett, M. (2015). *Future Sense*. London: Matador Books.

Parlett, M. (1997). The Unified Field in Practice. *Gestalt Review*, *1*(1): 16–33.

Perls, F.S. (1947). *Ego, Hunger and Aggression*. New York: Unwin Brothers Limited.

Perls, F.S., Hefferline, R.F., & Goodman, P. (1951). *Gestalt Therapy*. New York: Julian Press.

Petrie, N. (2013). *Vertical Leadership Development – Part 1 Developing Leaders for a Complex World*. Colorado: Center for Creative Leadership.

# REFERENCES

Polster, E., & Polster, M. (1973). *Gestalt Therapy Integrated*. New York: Vantage Books.

Siminovitch, D.E. (2017). *A Gestalt Coaching Primer*. Gestalt Coaching Works.

Siminovitch, D.E., & Van Eron, A.M. (2006). The Pragmatics of Magic: The Work of Gestalt Coaching. *OD Practitioner*, *38*(1): 50–55.

Simon, S. (2009). *Applying Gestalt Theory to Coaching*. Wellfleet: Gestalt International Study Center.

Simon, S. (2012). Applying the Cape Cod Model© to Coaching. *Gestalt Review*, *16*(3): 292–308.

Spoth, J., Toman, S., Leichtman., & Allan, J. (2013). Gestalt Coaching. In J. Passmore, D. Peterson, & T. Freire (Eds). *The Psychology of Coaching and Mentoring*. London: Wiley- Blackwell.

Yontef, G. (2002). The Relational Attitude in Gestalt Therapy. *International Gestalt Journal*, *25*(1): 15–35.

Zeigarnick, B. (1927). On Finished and Unfinished Tasks. *Psychologische*, *9*, 1–85.

Zinker, J. (1994). *In Search of Good Form*. San Francisco: Jossey-Bass.

# Index

*Note:* Page numbers in **bold** indicate tables on the corresponding pages.

action stage of Gestalt Cycle 67–68
Anderson, R. 79
assimilation and meaning-making stage of Gestalt Cycle 69–70, 135
attention, quality of 126
authenticity 78–79
awareness 12–13, 45–49; blocking 65; stage in Gestalt Cycle 65–66; structured awareness-raising processes 111–114

Backman, S. 37
balancing the strategic and intimate 37–40, **38**
Barber, P. 142
Beisser, A. R. 18
blockages, Gestalt Cycle 64–65; action stage 68; assimilation and meaning-making stage 70; awareness stage 66; contact stage 69; energy mobilisation stage 67; sensation stage 65
blocking awareness of new possibilities 65
Bohm, D. 105
both-and thinking 20

Carter, J. 9, 109
Casement, P. 87
Cason, K. 142–143
chairwork method 91–93
challenge 116–117

change: paradoxical theory of 18–19; transformational 27
check-in 26
compassion 135
*Comprehensive Guide to Vertical Development, A* 118
confirmation 78
confluence 61–62
contact 13, 51–54; confluence and 61–62; deflection and 60–61; desensitisation and 55–56; interruptions to 53–54; introjection and 56–57; noticing the quality of 128; patterns of 130–131; projection and 57–58; retroflection and 59–60
contact stage of Gestalt Cycle 68–69
contact-withdrawal patterns 52–53
context sensitivity 133–134
core principles in practice 81–83
core proposition 22
creative adjustment 21–24
creative experimentation 17, 91–96
Critchley, B. 142
cycle of experience 13–14

deflection 60–61
denial 65
desensitisation 55–56, 65
dialogic method 11, **12**, 77–80
dialogue: co-creation of 80; groups practicing 103–105; relational know-how for effective collaboration and 125–128

INDEX

either-or thinking 20
emerging needs 25
emerging process, working with 14
empathy 135
energy mobilisation stage of Gestalt Cycle 66–67
experiencing self 87
experiments: in group and team contexts 101–105; individually focused 97–99; unit of work as team learning 107–110

felt sense 34–35
field perspective 17–18, 33–35
figure-ground process 25–27, 95–96

Gendlin, E. 34–35
Gestalt approach 1–2; awareness in 12–13, 45–49; balancing the strategic and intimate in 37–40, **38**; benefits for coaches 4; conditions cultivated in 2; contact, and interruptions to contact in 13, 51–62; core proposition in 22; cycle of experience in 13–14; emergence of 7, **8**; field perspective in 17–18, 33–35; figure-ground process in 25–27; focusing on 'what is' 11–12, 29–32; health self-regulation and creative adjustment in 21–24; ideas and concepts in 2; intended readers of 3–4; main applications of 7–8; methodology of 2; more complex needs in 22; nature and power of unfinished situations in 41–44, **42**; paradoxical theory of change in 18–19; person in context in 33–35; phenomenological approach in 29–32; polarity thinking in 19–20; process orientation in 19; qualities of coaching relationship in 2; relational stance and dialogic method in 11, **12**, 77–80; skills and practices taught and passed on to clients in 3; in social and political contexts 10; working with emerging process in 14

Gestalt coaches: consulting and coaching programmes for 142; experiential workshops, ongoing personal growth groups, and communities of practice for 144; importance of personal development for 143; knowing their intentions and having a good sense of timing in interventions 139; personal study/reading for 144–145; recognising when they're triggered 137–138; recurring themes for training of 142–143; resisting over-structuring 138–139; training of 141; working creatively with 'resistance' 137; working with a Gestalt coach 143; working with a Gestalt supervisor 143

Gestalt Cycle *64*; action stage of 67–68; assimilation and meaning-making stage of 69–70; awareness stage of 65–66; blockages and resistances in 64–65; contact stage of 68–69; energy mobilisation stage of 66–67; sensation stage of 63

Gestalt in organisational, family, and community contexts **8**, 8–10

Gestalt practice: attending to the story and content whilst remaining attuned to process in 129; attuning to clients'

**151**

characteristic ways of responding and their contact patterns in 130–131; authenticity in 78–79; being fully present in the moment in 79; building trust and creating psychological safety in 75–76; confirmation in 78; core principles in 81–83; creating conditions for deeper personal development and connection in 73–76; creating the container for 73; creative experimentation and improvisation in 17, 91–96; cultivating 'context sensitivity' both in immediate and wider field in 133–134; dialogue engagement in 79–80; figure-ground process in 25–27, 95–96; Gestalt-based vertical leadership development programmes in 119–123; group and team context experiments in 101–105; guidelines for good 94–95; helping people learn how to complete units of work, assimilate learning, and make meaning in 135; holding space for 73–74; hold the space in 74–75; honing observational skills and sharing what you notice in 131–132; inclusion in 77–78; individually focused experiments in 97–99; intentional use of self in 14–15, 85–89; looking out for patterns in 82–83; relational know-how for dialogue and effective collaboration in 125–128; relational stance and dialogic attitude in 77–80; seeing everyone and not picking favourites in 82; staying with direct experience and intense emotional situations without seeking to shut down the client in 134; structured awareness-raising processes in 111–114; support, challenge, and dealing with complexity in 115–118; tracking issues and bringing unfinished material back to client's attention in 130; tuning in with empathy and compassion in 135; unit of work in 107–110; watch-outs for 137–139

Gestalt psychology **8**
Gestalt therapy **8**
ground 26, 27
group and team context experiments 101–105
group-think 61

Hanafin, J. 141
here and now, staying with 30–32
Hirsch, L. 9
holding space 73–74
horizontal learning 119–120

improvisation 17, 91–96
inclusion 77–78
individual coaching 9–10
intentional use of self 14–15
interpersonal capacity 125
interruptions to contact 53–54; confluence and 61–62; deflection and 60–61; desensitisation and 55–56; introjection and 56–57; projection and 57–58; retroflection and 59–60
introjection 56–57

Jaques, E. 142–143

keeping the lid on our unfinished situations 65
Kegan, R. 87

# INDEX

Leary-Joyce, J. 142
Lewin, K. 8–9, 18, 25, 34
lifeline sharing 113–114
life-space 18
listening for 126
listening to 127
Lukensmeyer, C. 9

management and leadership development 9
Mann, D. 96
Maslow, A. 21
meaning-making 69–70, 135
Melnick, J. 44, 49

Nevis, E. 9, 37
Nevis, S. M. 37, 44, 49
numbing out 65

observing self 87
organisational context **8**, 8–10, 37–39, **38**
organisational development (OD) 8, 34
*Organizational Consulting: A Gestalt Approach* 9
over-busyness 65

paradoxical theory of change 18–19
Parlett, M. 33
Perls, F. 93
permission to be creative 91
person in context 33–35
phenomenological approach 29–32
polarity thinking 19–20, 93
Polster, E. 44
Polster, M. 44
practitioner presence 14–15
presence, full 79, 85–86
process consulting 9–10
process orientation 19
projection 57–58
psychological safety 75–76

questions, asking more 127

receptive stance 14
relational stance 11, **12**, 77–80
resistances 64–65, 137–139
retroflection 59–60

self, the: developing the use of 88–89; intentional use of 14–15, 85–89
self-actualisation 21
self-awareness 46–47
self-development 87–89
self-regulation patterns 23
sensation stage of Gestalt Cycle 63, 65
sharing your own thinking 127–128
Siminovitch, D. E. 86
Simon, S. 75
social and political contexts, Gestalt in 10
social awareness 47–48
structured awareness-raising processes 111–114
support, emotional 23–24, 115

team coaching 9–10
tension as source of energy and motivation 42
tension systems 41–42, **42**
T-group methodology 9
timing of interventions 139
transformational change 27
triggers, recognition of 137–138
triumph, stories of 24
trust 75–76

understanding others' perspectives 127–128
unfinished situations 41–44, **42**, 65
unit of work 107–110, 135

verbal 360; feedback 111–112
vertical leadership development 117–118, 119–123

Wallen, R. 9

Zeigarnick, B. 41
Zinker, J. 91